Dare To Dream

Dare ᴛᴏ Dream

See Yourself as God Sees You

Paula White

New York Nashville

FaithWords
Hachette Book Group
1290 Avenue of the Americas, New York, NY 10104
faithwords.com
twitter.com/faithwords

Originally published in hardcover by FaithWords as *You're All That!*

This Edition: April 2017

FaithWords is a division of Hachette Book Group, Inc. The FaithWords name and logo are trademarks of Hachette Book Group, Inc.

The publisher is not responsible for websites (or their content) that are not owned by the publisher.

The Hachette Speakers Bureau provides a wide range of authors for speaking events. To find out more, go to www.hachettespeakersbureau.com or call (866) 376-6591.

Library of Congress Cataloging-in-Publication Data is available.

ISBNs: 978-1-4789-9184-7 (hardcover), 978-1-4789-9183-0 (ebook)

Printed in the United States of America

LSC-C

10 9 8 7 6 5 4 3 2 1

"*Men are all mosaics of other men.*"

—evangelist Henry Drummond

———————————

To everyone who has had a deep and profound impact on my life. It is your influence that has helped me on the journey to discern, develop, cultivate, and live out my authentic self.

CONTENTS

ACKNOWLEDGMENTS

Thanks to the friends, partners, and colaborers who dared to believe that together we can make a real difference, leave an indelible mark on mankind, and carry the cause of Christ on earth! A am forever grateful for our connection. Keep advancing . . . I believe in you!

INTRODUCTION

"Life is funny . . . You can't make it up."

—Momma

$\mathcal{M}$y mother's words to me were a simple explanation for the variables, unpredictable situations, and unforeseen events that would arise in this thing we call life. Would I be prepared for them? How would I respond? What would they do to me? How would the landscape of my life look after an unexpected event? Was I alone to figure it all out?

Every year I encounter masses of people who have lost something extremely valuable to them, and in the process they have lost a part of themselves. The loss may be a relationship, a career, or a home filled with warm memories. Invariably, what is lost on the outside includes a loss of identity on the inside—sometimes a loss so great the person is left wondering *Who am I? What is my value?* Many have never discovered the value of their authentic selves, who they really are, and therefore live life with false identities, with no real fulfillment or sense of purpose.

There are moments in our lives when we experience crises, distractions, violations, labels, victories, successes, and setbacks. You will probably agree that in this gift we call life, most of the decisive battles are fought from within. It is only when you confront yourself, remove the blinders, and deal with the real issues that have produced a "counterfeit" life that you can live the abundant life designed for you by a loving God.

Most people cheat themselves out of the rich rewards of this abundant, fulfilling, purposeful, and successful life by not asking the tough questions and by avoiding accountability. But sooner or later you must ask yourself, *Who am I, really? Am I living a life that is in alignment with my authentic self? Am I going in the right direction, or am I traveling all the time and seemingly getting nowhere? Is this what I really want to do with my life, or am I reacting to whatever comes from day to day? How will my life be lived out, and what will be my legacy?* Tough questions, yes, but worth asking in order to discover and receive the rewards of understanding and living God's design for your life.

I live a transformed and empowered life because I have discovered my original design, fashioned by the Master Architect Himself. I have learned that living through periods of pain and times of triumph is vital to finding out who we really are. It has been stated that I am a wounded healer—bold to proclaim to the world that God can and does heal all of our wounds. He causes the dark places of our soul to be healed so that not only can we function but we can soar.

As I began to work on this book, I sat down with my personal journals to review various periods of my life. I learned:

What you are willing to confront, God is willing to heal.
What you are willing to change, God is willing to grow.
What you are willing to leave behind, God is willing to
    transform.

God gives each of us highs and lows. We learn through them. We grow through them. And as we go through times of adversity and seasons of victory and emerge on the other side, if we trust in Him we discover more about who we are, who God is, and how God works.

My prayer is that this book will help you discover your uniqueness in God and locate the true person God created you to be and intends for you to become. No one can be you but you! I pray you will not only recover the truly valuable things that have been lost, but perhaps will also gain what has never been! I pray that you will discover the rare, original, magnificent, fabulous, beautiful person God designed you to be! You are one of a kind, irreplaceable, and valuable beyond measure. You truly are all that!

Dare To Dream

1

SELF . . . GONE MISSING

I stared at the empty crib in disbelief. Brad, not quite three years old, should have been lying there . . . and wasn't.

At first, I felt no great fear. This was too happy a day for that emotion to kick in immediately. It was the Fourth of July. Life was great! I had the day off, the sun was shining, a picnic and fireworks were planned for that afternoon and evening, the laundry was done and folded, and Brad was taking a nap so he'd have full energy for the festivities that were to come. I went to check on him, but he wasn't there!

Where did he go? Clever boy. He got out of his crib. Where is he now?

I called to him. No answer. I searched for him—under the bed, in every room, in every closet—even in the pantry. No Brad. I began to feel a sense of urgency.

Where is he?

How long has he been out of his bed?

Where should I look next?

I checked every window and door. All of them were securely closed and locked. Then I went to the patio door. I had recently moved into this apartment and had immediately installed a pinlock on the door, in addition to the regular patio-door locking mechanism. Both were high enough to be out of Brad's reach. To my tremendous surprise, the pin had been removed and the door was open several inches. It was at that moment that I felt panic!

I raced out the patio door, calling for Brad. The pool area was just beyond our patio, and because it was a holiday and the apartment complex was a large one, there were literally hundreds of people in and around that pool. I was frantic to find just one small person in a T-shirt and diaper! As loudly and as frantically as I called his name, nobody in that crowd of people seemed to hear me. They went on with their grilling and Frisbee-throwing and sunbathing. I felt such fear I could hardly breathe. I screamed his name even louder as I looked intently in every direction. I asked every person I could grab, "Have you seen my son? He's only two years old. He's missing!" Some people just stared back. Others shook their heads no. It was as if time had stopped, and this surreal moment of desperation had consumed me. This could not be happening to me.

I felt helpless, angry that nobody seemed to care, and frustrated that nobody had picked up a wandering baby and taken him someplace safe to wait for me. Mostly I felt tremendous and overwhelming fear. I rushed from person to person, calling for Brad, my eyes darting in every direction at once. Louder and louder I called, as I moved faster and faster through the crowd of people—all of whom seemed oblivious to my pleas and my frantic gestures.

This was my beloved baby! This was the most important person in the world to me! He was gone! *Didn't anybody have a heart to care?*

Finally a woman said, "Are you looking for a baby in diapers?" I cried, "Yes!" And she said, "He's over on the street corner."

I could hardly process her words. *Street corner?* The street corner was beyond the pool complex, beyond my apartment building and another large apartment building, and halfway down a busy street. I raced toward the street. When I got to the curb, I looked in both directions and spotted Brad standing on the corner, cars whizzing by. I raced to him, picked him up, and embraced him until I nearly suffocated him.

I carried him home, and trust me, he wasn't out of my sight for two seconds the rest of that day, week, and month! Once I came to my senses back in the apartment—after a flood of emotions that ranged from gratefulness to frustration to overwhelming love to self-recrimination—I began to question rationally and logically, "*How* did this happen?" And then, "*What* can I do to prevent this from happening again?"

New locks went on the doors, new safety mechanisms were put into place, including a sound monitor in his room, and mostly, a new level of understanding took root in me. A child nearly three years old must be guarded and monitored at *all* times. I had always been a watchful and careful mother, not simply in my own estimation but in the eyes of all who knew me. Yet now I became even more watchful and more careful.

I learned through this experience with Brad how devastating it can be to lose someone you love, even for a few minutes. But what if the person you lose is yourself? What if you have become so caught up in the busyness of life and in various relationships that you no longer know who you are, why you are on this earth, where you are going, or how to express yourself in a way that is authentic? What if you have never discovered or discerned that person . . . the real you?

As I have traveled the world in recent years, I have encountered countless people who have "gone missing." Some of them don't even know they are missing. They have lost all sense of self. I hear them say:

"I'm Lisa's mother."
"I'm a housewife."
"I'm Jeremy's grandma."
"I run a million-dollar company."
"I'm Fred's wife."
"I'm just a clerk at the company store."

They define themselves by external labels based upon associations and circumstances.

Others define themselves by the neighborhoods in which they live, or the cars they drive, or the labels on their clothing and accessories. Still others define themselves by the church they attend or the club to which they belong or the ministry outreach in which they participate. Labels and more labels, all external.

In the process of adding labels to their lives, and then defining themselves by those labels, these people have lost—or possibly never discovered—their own deep inner sense of self.

What do you *like?*
What do you *want?*
What do you *believe?*
What do you *envision?*
What do you *dream will happen in* your *future?*

Those who have lost a strong sense of personal identity often answer these questions with a blank expression. They have lived their lives according to the expectations, desires, preferences, and choices of others to the point that they truly don't know what they like, what they want, or what they dream. They walk through life as if on a treadmill. Busy days turn into busier days. Obligations and responsibilities continue to flow, until one day, the person is missing. The most basic question of all cannot be answered: *Who* are *you?*

If you don't really know who you are, can you answer:

When did you go missing?
What happened to chip away your identity?
How long have you been gone?
What prevented you from discovering your true self?
How do you rediscover yourself?
How do you find the authentic you?

You likely didn't lose your identity in a day, and you aren't likely to regain it in a day. There's a process involved, and a soul-searching that may be painful at times. The process involves:

Stripping away all the labels
Stripping away all the obligations and responsibilities
Stripping away all the relationships

And looking deep and long into yourself:

Who are you?
Who did God make you to be?
How can you live out His design, which is ultimately your fulfillment?

Very often, we come to that point of deep introspection in the wake of a loss. We may be grieving or in crisis. We may be facing what we consider to be the worst experience of our lives. And we come face-to-face with the reality that we have no inner identity on which to forge a new future.

Sometimes we come to that point of introspection when someone requires us to know who we are before they will continue a relationship with us. Sometimes we come to that point when we have a spiritual awakening, realizing that we have been created to live a life that we aren't living.

Whatever draws a person to ask the question, "Who am I?" is ultimately a good thing. Truly discovering and embracing the authentic you is one of the most exciting, rewarding, and life-changing journeys you can ever take. It is only in that place and position of discovery that you find your purpose and live your life completely.

"Who are you?" is the question this book invites you to ask.

It's the journey this book encourages you to pursue.

When you truly know who you are, all of life comes into focus.

*See Yourself
through
New Eyes*

2

DRILL TO THE CORE
OF YOUR IDENTITY

*H*i, my name is Paula," I said.

"I know who you are," the woman replied. "I know you very well. I watch you all the time on television. You're one of my best friends!"

I smiled. *She doesn't* really *know me,* I thought. But then I thought, *Or maybe she does!*

She certainly knows a part of me, because what you see is what you get when you see Paula. A man called me several months ago and said, "Are you for real?" I said, "I'm as real as I know how to be!"

In many respects, we human beings aren't all that different from each other. If we genuinely reflect our authentic selves, we can be known by others, and we can know others with greater insight. If we live from the core of our spiritual selves, we have "insider" information that spills over into "outsider" intuition and awareness.

Here are four things I know with absolute certainty about you:

I know you are a creation of God, made in His image. I know you are a one-of-a-kind unique design of God, who desires to be in relationship with you and help you live a fulfilling, wonderful, purpose-filled life. You have the personal challenge in your life of discovering who God made you to be and then living that life to the max.

I know that you are not on this earth merely to exist. You are here to live, with a kick in your step! God planned for you to be here—right now—with a purpose. He has ordered and is ordering your footsteps so that His plan and purpose for you might be fulfilled. God desires for you to rule and reign in life—and that starts by your ruling and reigning over your *own* life, and especially over your own thoughts and emotions.

I know that the core of you is stable. It doesn't change. It *is*. That core is spiritual. It is out of your spirit that your mind and emotions take shape. It is out of your mind and emotions that you speak and act. To know yourself fully, you must get in touch with your spiritual identity.

Real beauty is not outward. It is inward.

Real wealth is not outward. True riches are inward.

Real identity is not defined by outward trappings or labels. Real identity flows from the spirit deep within.

True reality lies in the realm of the unseen spirit deep within.

> True reality lies in the realm of the unseen spirit deep within.

I know that you are a multi-faceted jewel, highly valuable to God and capable of reflecting great beauty and light. I know that as you explore all of your own facets, you will have a greater desire and ability to see the beauty and uniqueness of other people.

I also know that we share many of the same desires—yes, even the same ultimate priorities—as creations of God.

WE SHARE SIMILAR DESIRES AND HAVE SIMILAR PRIORITIES

For the most part, we human beings have the same innermost desires and longings. The ultimate priorities of life are actually very few in number. What are they?

- The love of family and friends
- Assurance that we are in the best possible relationship with God
- Health, wholeness, and feelings of well-being—spiritual, mental, emotional, and physical
- Time for one more laugh, one more act of kindness, one more experience of beauty
- More faith
- A deep and fulfilling sense of purpose
- The opportunity to make a positive and eternal difference in the lives of others

These are not the things we put on resumés. They are not things we can buy off a shelf or even have custom-designed and manufactured. They are the things that satisfy the spirit, and they can be achieved only by spiritual means.

True success is living a life that satisfies your spirit with spiritual riches. Financial or material riches do not satisfy the spirit. Relationships and work do not satisfy the spirit. *Anything* superficial or external does not satisfy what is deep and internal. Furthermore, if you are not happy on the inside, there's nothing on the outside that will *make* you happy. If you don't feel that you are lovable, no amount of love showered upon you will *make* you feel loved.

> True success is living a life that satisfies your spirit with spiritual riches.

YOUR INDIVIDUALITY IS WORTH EXPLORING

All of the statements I've made above are true about you regardless of your age, gender, culture, tradition, or social standing. They are basic truths about human beings. Beyond these basics lie your individual traits, preferences, talents, dreams, personality, skills, and desires.

To a very great extent, the "you" that you see in your mind's eye is the "you" that you become. Who you think you are becomes who you are. The process flows from the inside out. If you know yourself spiritually, you know yourself authentically. And when you know yourself authentically, you can fully embrace all of the unique facets that make you *you*. You will see yourself as a person who is

- Valuable
- Lovable
- Capable
- Worthy of all that is good and eternal

Your perception of yourself is critical. If you don't see yourself accurately and positively, you need to discover the real you.

YOUR SELF-ESTEEM IS WORTH REEVALUATING

Every person has self-esteem. It's a matter of whether you have positive, high-quality, healthy self-esteem . . . or negative, low-quality, unhealthy self-esteem.

Here is the profile of a person who has positive, high-quality, healthy self-esteem:

- *Unconditional worth and value.* This person believes she is valuable regardless of what anyone else may say. Deep at her core, she has confidence that she is unique, precious, and eternal.
- *Love.* Every person needs love—warmth that radiates all the way to the innermost core of your being—and a healthy person has it. God is the greatest source of love a person can ever have. His love is infinite, constant, and continually flowing toward every one of His children. The second greatest source of love a person can ever know is not, as many people assume, the love of another person. It is the love a person has for herself. Only after a person embraces her unconditional worth and value can she truly receive love from someone else.

- *Growth.* Growth comes when a person gives herself to someone else, and that is what healthy people do. Nothing grows in a vacuum. It is only as a person gets out of herself, explores the world around her, and contributes to it out of her storehouse of love and talents that she can grow personally. The more she grows, the more she values herself. The more she gives away her love, the more worthy she sees herself to be. It is an upward spiral.

These three essentials for self-esteem are interdependent. The person who perceives herself to have high value is more willing to express love and, in return, to receive love. Such a person is more willing to help others in practical ways and to take risks to offer and provide help. The person who gives assistance and affection to others has higher regard for self.

Where are you in this process? Evaluate yourself!

You can begin to develop self-esteem at any point in the cycle. Start with believing you are worthy . . . or start by expressing love . . . or start by giving away your talents and time. All three aspects of self-esteem are designed by God to function simultaneously.

I have met people who believe that good self-esteem is contrary to godliness. Nothing could be further from the truth. God esteems us. He values us. He loves us. He declares us to be worthy of His mercy, forgiveness, and presence. He helps us to grow into the fullness of who He created us to be.

Our challenge is to esteem ourselves as God esteems us.

And the key is to see ourselves as He sees us.

DRILL DEEP—GET TO THE CORE

People in the oil business understand one very simple but essential truth: a person must drill for oil. Those who drill for oil sometimes have to drill deep, through layers of rock, to get to the oil their geological studies tell them is under the surface. At times the work is difficult and the process is long. But the rewards can be great!

Getting to your inner spiritual core . . .
Discovering all that you were created to be . . .
Changing your perceptions about yourself . . .

It can be difficult work, and it can take time. But the results and rewards are eternal. Drill deep, and don't give up.

3

CLEAR UP THE FUZZY PICTURE

*H*ave you ever seen a television set linked to an antenna—one that had a fuzzy, grainy, black-and-white picture? I certainly have. There were no cable systems, much less today's wireless technology, in the trailer park where I once lived. The image on that old television set was blurry and uninteresting, confusing and uninviting. Why? Because of faulty reception.

When we have faulty reception, we have unsatisfying and inaccurate perception. When we aren't fed accurate truths about ourselves, we develop a perception of self that is based upon lies, partial truths, and myths.

Today may be the day you need to adjust some of the dials on your life to get better reception. Today may be the day you need to change channels. Today may be the day you need to upgrade your old programs to new ones!

How you see yourself is absolutely critical. All self-appraisal begins with perception. Your perception is the basis for your self-identity and self-esteem. It is the foundation on which you build any relationship. Your self-perception gives rise to your choices and behavior. It is the predictor of your future prosperity and success.

If the perception that you hold of your own life is dull, you will act in a dull way, attract dull people, and live a dull life.

If the picture that you have of your own life is marked by failure, you will act in a way that sets you up for failure.

If the image that you have of your own worth is grainy and uninspired, you will act in a way that has no focus and no appeal.

How you *see* determines to a great extent who you will *be*.

CONQUERED BY LIFE OR CONQUEROR OF LIFE?

The Bible tells a story about twelve men sent to spy out the land God had promised to the Israelites when they left Egyptian slavery. After forty days of wandering through the land, all of the men came back with glowing reports about the fertility and produce they had seen. They described the land as "flowing with milk and honey" (Numbers 13:27). In other words, the grass was so lush that the cows couldn't help but produce milk in plentiful quantity, and the foliage was so thick that the honeybees had plenty to work with. They brought back pomegranates, figs, and grapes as proof of the land's bounty.

Two of the men said, "Let's go now! Let's move in and occupy the land God has given to us!" (see Numbers 13:30). These two men, Joshua and Caleb, focused on what God had promised to the Israelites and on what they believed God would do to enable them to conquer any obstacles ahead.

The other ten spies had a different take. They focused on the people they had seen in the land and they said, in essence, "We can't fight against these people. They are stronger than we are—in fact, they are giants." They made a statement that echoed through the next four decades: "We were in our own sight as grasshoppers, and so we were in their sight" (Numbers 13:33).

Fear gripped the Israelites. They refused to cross over into the land God had told them would be theirs. Instead, they wandered in a wilderness for forty years until every person *except* Joshua and Caleb died.

Victorious conquerors . . . or squashed grasshoppers.

Their fate lay in the way they saw themselves.

So, too, does your future flow from the way you see yourself. Your perception of yourself is far more powerful than the circumstances of your life. How others see you doesn't matter nearly as much as how you see yourself.

The way the majority of the Israelites saw themselves certainly wasn't the way God saw them. It wasn't the way Joshua and Caleb saw themselves or their fellow Israelites. But they saw themselves as failures, and they failed.

Joshua and Caleb saw themselves as successful, and they eventually succeeded. Joshua became the leader of the Israelites as they crossed the Jordan River forty years later to claim the land, defeating Jericho and countless other cities and areas. Caleb took possession of the hill country near Bethlehem and established roots in that region that continue until today (see Numbers 14:24, Joshua 1:1–11, and Joshua 14:6–14).

THOUSANDS OF PERCEPTIONS

There are countless perceptions available to you today. Choose the ones that line up with the Word of God. Discard the others.

Let me share with you two key principles about what you perceive. First, perception is about labeling and defining what you see, not with physical eyes but with inner eyesight. There is nothing absolute about perceptions. Perceptions are subject to interpretation. What one person perceives as excellent, another may see as merely so-so. What one person perceives as trash, another may see as art. What one person perceives as desirable, another may see as something to be shunned.

> Perceptions are all subject to interpretation.

The way we understand reality is influenced to a great extent by the definition that we give to the objects, behaviors, and experiences we encounter. We may call a ball red rather than green because we have come to define the color that we see as red. The truth is, the color of the ball is the color that we say it is—and in the case of colors, it is the color that people universally have agreed to say it is.

Second, we can be wrong in how we label what we perceive. What if your parents were colorblind? What if you were taught your colors incorrectly? What if nobody ever challenged you on your incorrect label or definition, but behind your back, people knew that you were incorrect? How would you know you were making a mistake? The only way you could know is if you came face to face with a reliable source that said to you, "This is the color *green,* not red."

When it comes to human behavior and our definitions of whether human behavior is good or bad, there is only one irrefutable, totally reliable source for labels and definitions: the Word of God. God's Word has stood the test of time—literally thousands of years. It is the only source that is truly worth consulting on matters of human behavior.

Millions have been taught wrong labels and definitions for their lives by people who did not first consult God's Word. Parents or other influential people may have said to a child, "You are bad. You are stupid. You are unwanted. You are not worthy of the air you breathe. You have no value and nothing to contribute."

If a child adopts those definitions and labels, he will act out of them as well. He will not try to act smart. Rather, he will embody the word *stupid.* He will settle for mediocrity and average or lower-than-average performance. He will allow others to mistreat him without challenging their behavior. And even as he embodies the labels he has been given, he will feel a deep-seated anger and frustration. Why?

Because this child was created by God, and God did not put these labels and definitions on this child or on any child. God's Word has the only true set of labels and definitions for every child: intelligent, worthy, valuable, lovable, capable, and redeemable!

The vast majority of frustrations and conflicts in this world today arise from one common source: a *lie* about who a person is and how a person should be treated.

YOUR PERCEPTIONS AND YOUR FEELINGS

The perceptions you hold about human experience, relationships, and identity are directly related to your emotions. How you feel is an indicator of what you perceive.

Are you uncomfortable in the presence of another person? What do you perceive about that person that gives rise to this feeling?

Are you relaxed and happy in the presence of another person? What do you perceive about that person?

Are you puzzled and confused in the presence of another person? Again, what perceptions cause you to experience those feelings?

Now take a moment to look at yourself. Are you frustrated by your own inabilities or failures?

Do you feel fearful?

Do you feel unlovable?

Why?

How do you perceive yourself?

YOUR PERCEPTIONS AND YOUR RELATIONSHIPS

To a very great extent, your perceptions of self drive your relationships. If you don't like the quality of people you hang out with, chances are you need to make some changes, first and foremost within yourself. You attract people who are similar to who you think *you* are. If you see yourself as a loser, you are likely attracting losers. If you see yourself as a winner, you are likely attracting winners.

Do you continually fall romantically for the wrong person? In all probability, this pattern is a reflection of the opinion you have of yourself. You are attracting the type of person that you think, even subconsciously, that you deserve.

We often try to change others so they might become who we *hope* they will be. Jesus addressed this tendency in the Bible. He said, in essence, "Don't try to take the splinter out of another person's eye. Deal with the log in your own eye" (see Matthew 7:4–5).

Deal with your self-perception! The more you begin to line up your self-perception with who God says you are, and the more you reflect the image God holds of you, the more likely you are to attract a quality person who will help you pursue the excellence that God desires for you. Such a person is likely to be someone you admire and respect!

PERCEPTIONS AND FEELINGS ARE SUBJECT TO CHOICE

Perhaps the most amazing principle related to perception is this: You have a choice about how you perceive yourself and the feelings you choose to hold in your heart.

Let me give you an example of this. A friend of mine told me recently about an afternoon that she spent with her mother. She said, "I went over to Mama's out of a feeling of obligation. I felt I should stop by and see her at least once or twice a week. I took her a bag of gingersnaps—her favorite—and sat down to help her pay her bills, which is something I do for her every month. Mama made a pot of tea and kept trying to feed me gingersnaps and tea while I worked on her bills. When I'd ask about a particular invoice, she'd respond in a way that seemed as if she was confused or not paying attention. I grew more and more frustrated, and no doubt because I was frustrated, she became more and more inattentive and confused. When she went to the kitchen, I found myself thinking, *You are giving me a headache!*

"Immediately, I felt ashamed of myself. I sat back and took a deep breath. I thought, *Sherill, you have a choice about how you are going to see your mother. She's seventy-nine years old and living alone. True, she's not as mentally sharp as she once was and her conversation meanders from one topic to the next. But you are focusing on her inabilities, not her abilities. Start seeing Mama as a warm, generous, hospitable woman who has the courage to make it on her own as a widow—a woman who still lives in her own house and takes care of herself, who delights in seeing her only daughter for a couple of hours a week.* Almost immediately, my feelings toward my mother changed. Feelings follow thoughts.

"I said to myself, *I'm going to love and appreciate the minutes I have left with Mama, whether those are fifteen years of minutes or just this week's minutes.*

I put away the bills and went over to the sofa with my cup of tea and two gingersnap cookies and we sat and talked for an hour. Mama was obviously delighted, and so was I. I chose to see my mother as a delightful tea-time companion and loving soul, and it was that perception that I held for the next seven years of her life, until the day she died. How I saw my mama made all the difference in the world, not only in the way I treated her and in the way we related to each other, but also in the way my children came to see her and relate to her, and in the way we now hold her in our memory."

Sherill's mama didn't change. Sherill's perception of her mother changed. And in the wake of that perception change, Sherill's feelings toward her mother changed.

Perceptions and feelings can always be changed, even the perceptions and feelings you have toward your self.

If you see yourself as being unworthy of good things, you will be miserable.

If you see yourself as incapable of making a positive choice in a situation, you will feel trapped and angry.

If you see yourself as a victim, you will feel despair.

If you see yourself as locked into a negative identity, you will lash out in negative ways that isolate you further.

If you see yourself as unlovable, you will exaggerate every act of kindness and hoard it with emotional stinginess.

How you see yourself determines how you feel. Therefore, if you don't like the way you feel, choose to feel differently. Choose to see yourself and others in a new way that is in alignment with God's Word!

> If you don't like the way you feel, choose to feel differently!

You *always* have a choice about how you perceive yourself and other people, and therefore, you *always* have a choice about:

- whether you will feel happy
- how you will respond to your circumstances
- how and in what manner you will exhibit hope, faith, and love

Will you choose to perceive yourself according to what others have said about you? Or will you choose to perceive yourself according to what God's Word says about you?

Choose to recognize and believe the true reflection of who you are. And if you don't know what God says about you? Find out!

4

SEE YOURSELF AS
GOD SEES YOU

I'm scared of God," she said.

"You wouldn't be if you knew God," I said. "You'd love Him."

"How do you know that?" she asked.

"Because He loves you with a huge and lasting love, and that kind of love is utterly irresistible."

"I'm angry with God," he said.

"You wouldn't be if you knew God," I replied. "You'd be grateful at discovering that He is on your side all the time."

"I'm not even sure I believe in God," he countered.

"He believes in you," I said. "That's what really matters."

Time and again, I encounter people who assume that God sees them as worthless throwaways, sinners deserving to be cast into the nearest hellfire, or the recipients of His awesome wrath and punishment. The truth is, God does not see you or anyone else that way. He sees you as His beloved creation, with whom He desires to spend all of eternity.

I also encounter people who, because they have a faulty perception about God, continually strive to have enough, do enough, or be good enough to sidestep God's vengeance and gain God's approval. They don't understand that God does not evaluate anyone on the basis of things external or behavioral. God does not see you or any other person through the lens of a bank account, a family tree, a job, a performance, a title, social standing, or a set of accomplishments.

A great challenge we all face is to see ourselves as God sees us. And that's the key to getting our spiritual identity in sharp focus!

YOU BY ANY OTHER NAME . . . IS *YOU!*

We've all heard the Shakespeare-inspired phrase, "A rose by any other name is still a rose." The truth is also, "You by any other name . . . is *you.*" Your name, in Bible terms, is much more than the name your parents gave you at your birth.

The Bible tells about a man named Jacob who wrestled with God (Genesis 32:24–32). During the wrestling match, God asked Jacob, "What is your name?" Certainly God already knew Jacob's name. A name, however, meant much more at that time than it means today. Parents named their children according to very specific traits or insights they had into their children's future. To name someone was to give him identity and to exert a certain degree of control over the expression of that identity. When Adam named the animals in the Garden of Eden, for example, he wasn't just assigning labels to the animals—he was comprehending and describing their natures, their behaviors, their activities, their personalities. God knew Jacob's identity—his nature—but He asked this question so that Jacob might confront his identity. Jacob answered the way he had been taught to answer all of his life: "Jacob."

The name Jacob means "supplanter"—somebody who takes something that isn't his, or lays claim to something that doesn't fit him or belong to him, usually by some sort of unfair manipulation. To be a supplanter is to be a deceiver, a trickster, a manipulator, a swindler. The name "supplanter" was given to Jacob because he came out of his mother's womb holding on to his twin brother's heel. From birth, Jacob was someone who laid claim to things that weren't his—the rights of the firstborn.

Jacob internalized that definition of supplanter for his life. He saw himself the way others saw him. As a young man, he tricked his brother Esau into giving him his birthright—the right to the inheritance that belonged to the firstborn. Jacob wasn't satisfied, however, with supplanting only this in Esau's life. He also tricked his father Isaac into giving him the blessing that was intended for the firstborn. As a result, Jacob literally had to run for his life, and he ended up in his uncle Laban's home. Laban was a supplanter if ever there was one! Jacob ended up marrying both Leah and Rachel as the result of a trick his uncle played on him, and he worked fourteen years for Laban as the consequence of that trick.

The day came when Jacob left Laban. And—no surprise—he did it in a tricky way! He stole away without saying goodbye, fleeing Laban's home with his wives, children, servants, possessions, flocks, and herds. When he got to the Jabbok River, Jacob divided his great entourage of people and animals into two groups in anticipation of an encounter with Esau and his family. He was thinking like a trickster even as he made his way home after many years' absence. He calculated that if Esau saw only half of his family and herds, he would be more inclined to accept Jacob's presence in the territory, and if Esau sought to kill Jacob's family and animals, at least he'd kill only half. Jacob's manipulative, scheming mind was functioning in full gear!

Jacob sent all that he had across the brook and spent the night alone at the river's edge, and there God wrestled with him until dawn. During the wrestling match, Jacob's hip was pulled out of its socket, but Jacob did not let go of God even in the pain of that experience. At daybreak, the Lord said to Jacob, "Let me go," and Jacob said, "Not until you bless me."

I want you to notice several very important things about this story:

A PERSONAL AND PRIVATE MATTER

First, Jacob was alone that night in the wilderness. He had done everything he knew to do. He was at the end of what he could control. And he separated himself from all his family and belongings and work for that night.

The very essence of self-discovery is seeing yourself apart from all other relationships and responsibilities. The "core you" is the you that exists even if you aren't somebody's parent, child, spouse, employer or employee, pastor, physician, caregiver, helper, friend, and so forth. If you truly want to discover your self-identity, you need to see yourself as you are *by yourself*.

> The very essence of self-discovery is seeing yourself apart from all other relationships and responsibilities.

As you seek to discover who God says you are, you will benefit greatly from retreating to a place where you can be alone with God. It may be just for a night, as in Jacob's case, or for a weekend or a week, or even longer. I know a woman whose husband left her for another woman. After dealing with some of the very practical matters related to the care of her children and her home, she asked her parents to take her children for a few days, and she flew to one of her favorite places—a beach setting where she had spent happy days in her childhood. She went to the beach early in the morning and at sunset, taking long walks and talking to God.

She said, "I discovered myself again on those walks. I saw the ebb and flow of life so clearly as the waves lapped up on that beach. I saw the way the ocean washed the beach clean at high tide. I asked God to wash my life in that way and not allow me to clutter it up again with bad choices and decisions. I came away with renewed hope, more energy, and a much clearer perspective."

What this woman experienced is what many people experience when they can get away by themselves for a while. I have a personal retreat place where I go to be alone with God. It's where I do my best Bible study and where I have prepared some of my most effective sermons. It's a place where I can rest and feel creative at the same time. I don't spend prolonged periods there, but I do spend the time I need so that I am able to keep a clear focus on who I am as an individual in God, and to gain the rest and restoration needed for the incredibly busy, complicated life I lead. When we know who we are individually in God, it gives us a tremendous opportunity to express ourselves in new ways to each other—to connect at even deeper levels and to strengthen our love for the people in our lives.

I often say, "What makes a great relationship is when I am free to be me, you are free to be you, and together we can determine who we are."

Getting alone with God is not an escape. It's a way to confront what we need to confront and to grow!

A WRESTLING MATCH

The Bible says that Jacob wrestled with God. Will time spent alone with God always result in a wrestling match? No! But a wrestling match of sorts is likely to take place if you think that in getting away by yourself, you are getting away from everything else, including God. The truth is, you can never get away from God. It is important that you recognize that when you seek to spend time *by yourself,* you are also spending time *with God.* If you attempt to discover yourself without factoring God into the equation, He is likely to show up and confront you, just as He did Jacob.

"But," you may be saying, "God is scary. I'm not sure I can handle being alone with God." Let's deal with that. Being scared of God is not grounded in anything He has done to you or failed to do for you. It comes from a distorted perception of God. When a person is scared of God, it is usually because somebody in her past taught her to be scared of God. Or it is because God has been given a bad rap—He has been blamed for something perceived as negative.

God has revealed His nature in His Word. From cover to cover in your Bible, you will find that God loves His children and seeks their highest and best good, not only now but for all of eternity. The apostle Paul described God's nature as having these hallmarks in addition to love: joy, peace, patience, kindness, goodness, faithfulness, gentleness, and self-control (Galatians 5:22–23).

"But," you may be saying, "if God is all that, why doesn't He keep bad things from happening to good people?"

While God can prevent or cause anything to happen that He desires, He has also given us a big dose of free will. God does not force us to make the vast majority of decisions that we make, and He does not *keep* us from making errors or bad choices. We must take responsibility for those things that arise from our own choices and decisions.

We also need to recognize that we live in a fallen world. We live in a world troubled by fierce storms and erupting volcanoes. We live in a world shaken by earthquakes and wars. We live in a world full of terrorists, drug dealers, child abusers, murderers, thieves, and all sorts of other dishonest, hell-bent, angry, rebellious, bitter people—each of whom also has a measure of free will that can be exercised for good or evil.

God does not snatch us out of this world and put a protective coating around us. He tells us in His Word that He walks through this life with us, never leaving us or forsaking us. But nowhere in God's Word will we find a promise that He will spare us all hardship. He does promise not to allow any form of evil to strip away our salvation, our home in eternity, or our ability to experience God's presence in our soul. I have found that faith doesn't necessarily stop all bad things from happening, but it does carry us through them. In fact, greatness is often birthed from the adversities in our lives.

Instead of blaming God for what has—or hasn't—happened to you, thank God for who you are right now and for who you are becoming.

Never lose sight of the fact that you are the created; He is the Creator.

You are finite; He is infinite.

You are bound by time and space; He is eternal and ever-present.

You know things in part; He knows everything in full.

We are wise when we welcome the presence of God into our lives. We are wise when we consult God about who we are and what He has planned for us. The truth is, we can never escape the fact that we are His creation and He is the Creator. And although I don't understand every life event, I have graduated from faith to trust, knowing that He is a good God who *always* has my best interests in mind. I have learned by experience to trust His heart even when I don't understand His plan.

God loves and cares about you far beyond human comprehension.

There isn't anything about you that God doesn't know. He built into you every facet of your personhood and He knows your history, your present, and your future. Perhaps that is why we are commanded in His Word to praise Him in all things and for all things. Our attitude in the midst of trials reveals our understanding of the character of God. We can be totally honest with God.

To the extent that you are transparent before God, He will reveal more and more of Himself to you and show you more and more about who He made you to be as part of His greater plans and purposes. According to Romans 8:28, God takes all things—including things that can damage our well-being—and turns them into good. Learn to rest in that fact!

Seek to know God.

Seek to discover what God knows about you!

Come to the place where you are willing and eager to see yourself through God's eyes.

It wasn't easy for Jacob to accept that God had more control over his life than he had, or to give up trying to manipulate things in his favor. Jacob had to come to grips—literally!—with the presence and power of God in order to know and accept who he was in God's sight.

> Come to the place where you are willing and eager to see yourself through God's eyes.

Jacob learned five important truths about God. If you are uncertain about these facts, you need to understand them!

- *God is real.* He exists. He is present at all times. Nothing you can do is hidden from God. He knows you thoroughly.
- *God is personal.* He has numbered the hairs on your head (see Matthew 10:30). He knows every experience you've had. He is intimately familiar with all of your excellent traits and all of your unfulfilled dreams and desires.
- *God is in control.* Nothing that happens to you is a surprise to God. Because God is omnipotent, He can change things and adjust things at any time, in countless ways. He is able to turn all negative

experiences in your past to positive experiences in your future (see Romans 8:28).

- *God wants to relate to you.* He longs to communicate with you, to be consulted by you, to walk with you on life's journey, to forgive you. He longs for you to depend on Him for everything in your life. He wants an intimate relationship with you.
- God desires what is eternally best for you. God is love. He is good. He is your provider, protector, redeemer, deliverer, savior, and the sure foundation that does not fail.

Jacob's encounter with God was not all serenity or a walk in the park. For Jacob, the encounter was real—it was painful—it was intense. A wrestling match is not a life-or-death struggle, but it nevertheless is a struggle. To wrestle with something is to engage it in order to know and understand it.

I know this from my own experience with abuse, emotional pain, and addictive behavior: if you have acquired an identity that does not match up with who God designed you to be, or if you have acquired a wrong understanding of God's nature, your journey to a correct self-identity is going to involve a struggle. The more off-kilter your self-concept, or the more out-of-whack your concept of God, the more intense the struggle will be.

You may have a lot of unlearning to do.

You may have a lot of changes to make in your thinking.

You may have a lot of new learning to pursue.

Don't expect the realignment of your self-concept or your God-concept to come easily. But do expect it to come. Just as we see in the example of Jacob wrestling with God until morning light, do expect that God will not let go of you until you make it to dawn!

A NIGHT OF CHANGE

Jacob was never the same after that night. It was a fork in the road of his entire life.

Jacob didn't change God. God changed Jacob.

It's important to recognize that Jacob didn't win his wrestling match with God. He couldn't trick God, out-smart God, or supplant God. He couldn't have his way in this matter. He couldn't change God, but God could change him. The same is true for you. So many people think they can make it on their own without any help, influence, or constraints from God. But that simply isn't possible. The reality is that life is too big for you to carry the burden on your own shoulders. In 1 Peter 5:7, God's Word says to cast all your cares upon God. He can handle the heavy weights that wear you down in life. He can handle your issues and love you unconditionally. You can stand before Him confident and unashamed.

When you don't rely on or trust in God for your life, you are marked by utter rebellion and pride. In truth, you can't make your own heart beat another beat. You can't force your lungs to breathe another breath. You can't jump from a hundred-foot cliff and land gently on your feet. Neither can you leap off that cliff and fly. You are intricately connected to God and His creation, and He longs to have a relationship with you.

By ignoring God, you grieve His heart, and ultimately you hurt yourself.

By diminishing the role of God in your life, you don't demean God. You limit yourself.

When you deny the power of God, you don't destroy God. You put yourself on a path of living that is inferior to the life He has designed for you.

When you acknowledge God, yield to God, honor God, and exalt God, it greatly enhances your own life, both your well-being and your eternal future.

Jacob had no lasting influence on God that night, but God exerted a lasting influence on Jacob, one that extended to his heirs.

The Bible says that in the wrestling match, God touched the socket of Jacob's hip so that it went out of joint (see Genesis 32:25). Jacob came out of this experience with a limp. He could still walk, and he did. But he had an ever-present reminder that God was the Creator of his identity and his destiny.

A "limp" is not a weakness but a strength—an understanding of who you really are. I would not want to be intimately connected to someone who doesn't "walk with a limp." Jeremiah 17:5 says, "Cursed be the man that trusteth in man, and maketh flesh his arm, and whose heart departeth from the Lord." Your limp shows me that you have learned to yield your life to God. And because of that, true life, power, and provision flow from you.

God changed the way Jacob walked, and God changed the way Jacob viewed himself and presented himself to other people.

I would like to be able to tell you that your bad experiences can be totally erased from your memory, but that would be a lie. In truth, we never fully forget anything this side of eternity. Our brains store things in subconscious memory even if we cannot recall them with our conscious mind. God created our minds with the ability to learn from past mistakes so we won't make those mistakes again. We can avoid making decisions that lead us into painful or destructive patterns. We are covered and healed by the love, grace, and mercy of God so that former experiences have no effect on our current life.

I have preached for many years that "God wants to scar you." Some people interpret that incorrectly to mean that God wants to injure a person so the person will be scarred up. Nothing could be further from the truth! The message is this: God wants to heal your deep, gaping, painful, ugly wounds so that only a scar remains.

I have a large scar on one knee. It is a reminder to me that I once had a terrible fall that resulted in a horrific wound. But today, this scar is only a reminder of that experience. The scar certainly doesn't hurt like the wound did. The scar doesn't provide an opportunity for infection like the open sore did. And it's a good reminder to watch where I run! In the same way, the emotional wounds that have been inflicted upon your life can be healed so that you remember what happened, but you no longer feel the searing pain associated with what caused them.

A wounding is an event. A scar is a reminder of that event, but without the pain.

Another thing God changed about Jacob during their encounter was Jacob's name—his identity. Jacob was desperate for God's approval. He said to God, "I won't let You go unless You bless me" (see Genesis 32:27)! Jacob didn't want to merely survive that night. He wanted something *good* to come out of it.

Always go to God expecting to come away with something good. This is a critical point—God doesn't call you apart to encounter Him and to encounter yourself with the intention of hurting you, destroying you, or showing you all of your faults. No way! He wants to show you who you really are: fearfully and wonderfully made by God Himself (see Psalm 139:14). You are distinct, rare, original, marvelous.

God doesn't belittle you, criticize you, or reject you when you ask Him to reveal who you are, why He made you, and what He desires for you to become and do on this earth. In fact, the Bible says that if a person goes to God in search of wisdom, God will pour out His wisdom generously and without any finger-pointing or fault-finding (see James 1:5).

Go to God expecting Him to reveal both His absolute goodness and your potential for greatness. God desires for you to live in such a way that you will reflect Him—and He is glorious, excellent, unmatchable in His perfection. If you grow into a reflection of such an awesome God, you can't help but share in His glorious, excellent, unmatchable nature. That's His promise. Go to Him expecting that to occur—not overnight, but eventually. It's His plan for you (see Romans 8:29–30).

A NEW IDENTITY

Let's go back to the point where God asked Jacob his name. Jacob replied, "Jacob." In one translation of the Bible, it says that Jacob spoke "in shock of realization, whispering" (Genesis 32:27 AMP). Jacob could not escape the truth of his own identity at that point. In coming face-to-face with God, Jacob came face-to-face with himself.

God responded, "Your name shall no longer be called Jacob, but Israel" (see Genesis 32:28). The name *Israel* literally means "contender." Contenders have power. If you go into a boxing match, you are only a contender if you have the potential for prevailing. Contenders garner attention. They are heard. They are recognized as worthy.

The word *contender* is translated in some Bible versions as "one who prevails." The simple truth is that you can't prevail unless you contend . . . and if you contend long enough, you will prevail!

What does it mean to prevail with God? Success with God always means that you choose to do things God's way, not your own way. God's ways are not meant to be harsh or difficult, as some might think. You can trust that God has designed an abundant life for you that is released through your obedience to Him.

God's directives may be as simple as a prompting in your mind: "Call this person today." It might be a leading to make a particular choice or to go to a particular place at a specific time. When we do what God directs us to do—trusting that He alone can see the beginning and the ending of our lives and knows every step along the way—we walk in confidence that He is leading us, guiding us, and taking us down paths that are truly good for us.

> Success with God always means that you choose to do things God's way, not your own way.

Choosing to do things God's way means that we accept God's plan of forgiveness for our lives, knowing that it is a great plan to lead us into His promises.

Choosing to do things God's way means that we see ourselves as He sees us, and we begin to take on our identity as His beloved, righteous, and forgiven children, no longer living under guilt, shame, and punishment.

Choosing to do things God's way means that we ask Him for help in everything, from giving up a bad habit to adopting a positive new discipline.

Choosing to do things God's way means that we present ourselves to others as people who love God, and therefore love others with life-transforming love.

The person who does this becomes a person who not only prevails with God, but who is a winner to herself and to other people. She rises above daily circumstances and even the most negative of situations. She finds a way to meet needs, soars above verbal assaults, and leads a life of genuine integrity and authenticity.

When you know that you are a contender and a prevailer, you begin to adopt the stance—emotionally, spiritually, and mentally—that "I am a valuable person, successful in the eyes of the One whose opinion truly matters." Your shoulders go back, you hold your head high, your eyes are focused and direct, your handshake is firm, and your walk is confident.

I frequently find myself in major cities all over the world, and I have become a people-watcher. I can tell you a great deal about a person just from seeing how she carries herself when she walks and by watching her interact with at least one person. Our core identity is expressed to the outside world in those moments when we don't think anybody is watching us or evaluating us.

When God changed Jacob's name to Israel, Jacob was no longer "trickster" but "contender/prevailer." What a difference this change in name and identity made to Jacob from that moment on! What a difference it will make in your life when you hear deep within your spirit who you *really* are in God's eyes!

Jacob didn't have to *strive* to gain power. God already saw him as worthy of accomplishment and success.

Jacob didn't have to *struggle* to prove himself. God already granted him status.

Jacob didn't have to *scheme* to acquire what he desired. God already saw him as a person deserving of life's best.

And so it is for you!

RELATIONSHIP, NOT DEEDS

For much of his life, Jacob defined himself by his behavior. He played tricks, concocted schemes, and manipulated and maneuvered himself to the place he wanted to be. But God defined Jacob according to his relationship with God.

It is critical for you to understand this concept. We tend to see ourselves in light of what we have done. If we've had a string of failures or dysfunctions in our life, we are likely to conclude, "I'm not any good." We call ourselves "stupid," "worthless," "average," "less." We may not say these words aloud to others—although I'm amazed that some people do call themselves failure-related names in the presence of others—but we certainly think these words to ourselves. God says to us, "You may have done some stupid things, you may have failed at times, but you are not stupid or a failure." Who you are and what you have done are not the same. Being and doing are two separate things. Your behavior can contradict the authentic you if you have a faulty belief system. God sees you in relationship to Himself—and that is how you need to see yourself.

You are His forgiven child.

You are His beloved.

You are His cherished one.

You are His masterpiece creation.

You are the apple of His eye.

GIVE YOURSELF A NEW NAME

I strongly encourage you to adopt a new name for yourself at some point. You may be most comfortable making this a new nickname for yourself, perhaps by adding an adjective to your name. I like thinking of myself as "Passionate Paula" and "Purposeful Paula." I don't use these names in public, but I do call myself by these names when I talk to myself in the mirror!

What a difference it makes when a person comes to see himself or herself as:

- Forgiven Fred
- Beloved Belinda
- Strong Steve
- Cherished Cheryl
- Great Gary
- Jubilant Janet
- Super Sam
- Terrific Tawanda

What new name might you have, based upon your relationship with God and your discovery of your authentic self?

The Bible says that when the apostle John was imprisoned on the isle of Patmos, he had visions, and in one of them, he was given a specific message for each of the major churches in Turkey at that time. One of those messages from God stated that He was going to give two things to those who "overcame evil": hidden manna to eat, and a white stone with a new name written on it, which no person would know beyond the person who received the stone (see Revelation 2:17).

In the book of Revelation, *manna* refers to spiritual food—nourishment that gives spiritual energy and strength. Spiritual nourishment produces spiritual zeal and fortitude. Only God can truly give spiritual nourishment. People may try a thousand ways to nourish their own spirits, change their own spirits, or create their own spiritual energy and strength. But these things don't happen by human effort. They happen only as God infuses each person with Himself. God invites us to say yes to Him, and when we do, He imparts Himself to us.

The white stone mentioned in Revelation is a symbol that means "yes." In casting lots, white stones are a "yea," black stones a "nay." A white stone is a mark of affirmation, of being chosen, of being worthy of selection. The name etched into stone means that this new name is permanent—solid, fixed, established. When a person seeks God and discovers his or her identity in God, that "new-name identity" is lasting.

What is it about you that deserves a "yes"—a shout of affirmation that declares, "This is truly who I am"? That's your core nature. It's God-established, God-revealed, God-honored.

Identify yourself by the new name—the core identity, the true you—that He reveals to you as you explore your authentic self, read His Word, and pray.

Learn to live in the authenticity of that identity!

5

EVALUATE YOUR LIFE AND FUTURE ON GOD'S TERMS

One day during a difficult time in my life, I got in my car and drove to the beach. I sat there, cell phone off, and made this a purposed time for deep contemplation about who I was in Christ. I began to list the various traits that the Bible identifies as my identity in Christ, and next to each trait I put down the Bible verse where that trait is given. The list I made appears below. These are traits that are true for every person who has accepted Jesus as her Savior.

THE BELIEVER IN CHRIST JESUS IS:

- Fearfully and wonderfully made—Psalm 139:14
- God's workmanship, created in Christ Jesus—Ephesians 2:10
- Victorious—Revelation 21:7
- Called by God—2 Timothy 1:9
- More than a conqueror—Romans 8:37
- Ambassador for Christ—2 Corinthians 5:20
- Beloved of God—1 Thessalonians 1:4

- Joint-heir with Christ—Romans 8:17
- Overtaken with blessings—Deuteronomy 28:2
- Complete in Christ—Colossians 2:10
- Firmly rooted, built up, and strengthened in faith—Colossians 2:7
- Enabled to do all things—Philippians 4:13
- Always triumphant—2 Corinthians 2:14

The Christian's self-esteem is ultimately that person's individual judgment about her worthiness in Christ. Her reputation lies in the truth that she has been saved and belongs to God, that she has been equipped in Christ to face any situation of life and overcome it, and that she is lovable because God first loved her. She has been forgiven of *all* past sins and is not a product of her past. She is capable of walking in newness of life because the Holy Spirit has promised to be with her constantly—to help, guide, and teach her all that she needs to know to live a life of tremendous reward. She can experience satisfaction in life and be of benefit to others (see Galatians 6:4 and 2 Peter 1:2–4).

THREE GREAT TRUTHS ON WHICH TO BUILD YOUR LIFE

The Bible isn't a book of opinions. It is truth, from cover to cover. There are three biblical truths on which you can build a solid, stable, satisfying life:

- God is in control—all the time.
- God is eternal, and the things He does are lasting.
- God gives us free will to choose happiness.

God Is in Control

God is God, and there is no one like Him. Nothing is beyond His influence or control. There is no sin that He cannot forgive if the person is willing to be forgiven. There is no relationship He cannot mend if both persons are willing to come into alignment with His principles. There is no obstacle that He cannot remove, change, or overcome. There is no flaw that He can't mend. There is no challenge too great. There is simply nothing too difficult for God.

God Is Eternal, and the Things He Does Are Lasting

God says about any person's life that it isn't over until He says it's over. Nothing in this life, therefore, is permanent until death. All situations and circumstances are subject to change, and all are subject to God.

Take a few minutes to think about what you have just read. *Nothing* you are facing is permanent. Every situation on this earth is temporary. Life is unfolding, developing, changing, and being altered "behind the scenes," even when you don't perceive any change. God is always at work. He doesn't sleep or slumber, and He is always designing, refining, and bringing about the highest good for His beloved children.

> Every situation on this earth is temporary. Life is changing . . . even when you don't perceive any change.

God Gives Us Free Will to Choose Happiness

There is a great deal of confusion about happiness in our world today. We have convinced ourselves as a society that things make a person happy. Virtually every commercial on television promises a degree of happiness to the person who will purchase the product being sold. We have convinced ourselves that we have a "right" to be happy—and that if we will only put ourselves into the right relationship at the right time with the right stuff stacked around us, we will be happy.

But the truth is, there is no "happiness formula" associated with material goods or external circumstances. There is no permanent state of happiness to which a person can move.

Happiness is not *happen*-ness. Happiness is not automatically linked to a particular event or circumstance. It is a matter of perception, a choice. The Bible says that all things work together for good for those who love God and choose to put themselves in alignment with His purposes (see Romans 8:28). Therefore, you can choose to believe that everything that happens to you is a factor in creating your ultimate good. You can choose to be happy in a situation or circumstance, even a dire or undesirable circumstance. Why? Because you aren't drawing your happiness from the event or situation itself, but rather, you are drawing happiness from your belief that God is always at work and that He will create something good for you.

> Happiness is not happen-ness. Happiness is not automatically linked to a particular event or circumstance.

GAIN A GLIMPSE OF YOUR FUTURE PROSPERITY

I don't define prosperity in terms of money or material objects. I define it in terms of "fruitfulness." A prosperous life is a life that is fruitful physically, mentally, emotionally, and spiritually. The fruitful person is healthy, creative, emotionally strong, and spiritually alive and sensitive. She meets the needs of others and produces high-quality, beneficial work. She loves others and trains up the next generation in things that are good, noble, and lasting. The fruitful person leaves a rich legacy of character and influence.

Your perception of who you are in Christ and your perception about who God is are the best predictors I know of your future prosperity.

The Word of God tells us that the way a person *thinks* about himself is the predictor of what the person *becomes* (see Proverbs 23:7).

The Bible also teaches that the way a person *thinks* is the foremost predictor of what the person *possesses*. A person subconsciously attracts what he believes he deserves.

A DAILY REMINDER TO SELF

I encourage you to begin each day by reminding yourself:

- I am a child of God.
- I am blessed by God.
- I am loaded with benefits today according to God's Word.
- I am on the way to experiencing the fullness of the success God has for me.
- God will not withhold any good thing from me.
- God will meet my needs.
- I will live in the fullness of God's wholeness, experiencing true prosperity because He provides for me.

When you expect good things from God, you will be quicker to reach out and grab hold of the opportunities that come your way. Just as important, when you see yourself as a person of tremendous quality and value, you will seek out and appreciate things that are of high quality and value. If you see yourself as deserving only a stale crust of bread, you will reach for that instead of a soft yeast roll or a croissant. If you see yourself as worthy only of a rattletrap car, you will be satisfied with that instead of asking for, working for, or looking for the best deal on a better set of wheels. If you see yourself as worthy only of a shabby apartment in a crime-infested area, you will settle for that, instead of setting your sights on the training that will get you a well-paying job so that you can afford to live in a nicer place in a safer neighborhood.

People who have strong self-worth take care of their possessions and homes. They present themselves with more style and keep their personal possessions cleaner and in better repair. As a result, they attract others who also have higher self-worth and who take increased care of their belongings.

You will not violate what you value. What you perceive yourself to be worthy of having, you will eventually have. You are worthy of *all* God's blessings.

BELIEVE FOR GOD'S BEST

Having nice things is not at all contrary to a godly life. There are a number of mixed messages in the Christian world about material goods and finances. Some believe that God desires for people to be poor; this belief fits their concepts of humility and dependence on God. The Bible, however, does not call all people to poverty. Others believe that God bestows riches on those who are holy; this fits their concepts of blessing and abundance. The Bible, however, does not promise all people great financial riches.

What the Bible does teach is that God supplies the needs of His people. He delights in bringing people to a wholeness in life that includes physical, spiritual, mental, emotional, relational, material, and financial sufficiency for all things He has called them to do (see Philippians 4:19). To be whole is to have vibrant energy and freedom, which enables a person to move obediently, quickly, and enthusiastically in whatever direction the Lord leads.

God's blessings to us include meeting our practical and daily needs. The Bible says, "Blessed be the Lord, who daily loadeth us with benefits" (Psalm 68:19). Jesus taught His disciples to pray, asking their heavenly Father to "give us this day our daily bread" (Matthew 6:11). The Bible tells us that we are to ask for our material provision, and that we often don't receive all that we need because we do not ask God for it (see James 4:2).

The balance in this is that we are to ask with faith, we are to use what we receive in a way that promotes wholeness, and we are to receive what God gives to us with great joy (see James 1:6–7 and 1 John 5:14). The Bible also teaches that we are to respond to God's gifts with thanksgiving (see Psalm 106:1). We are to share generously with others (see Proverbs 22:9), and we are to seek spiritual blessings (see 1 Corinthians 14:1–12).

Health, success, salvation, inner peace, loving relationships—all of these are part of the total package that God desires to give to those who love and serve Him (see 3 John 2). Don't limit yourself in trusting God for his highest, best, and most complete blessing. He seeks to give you a life that is abundantly overflowing, more than anything you can imagine (see John 10:10 and Ephesians 3:20). God's Word promises very real and tangible success to those who trust in Him and obey Him. Read these three verses from Psalms:

> Trust in the LORD, and do good; so shalt thou dwell in the land, and verily thou shalt be fed.
> Delight thyself also in the LORD; and he shall give thee the desires of thine heart.
> Commit thy way unto the LORD; trust also in him; and he shall bring it to pass.
>
> (Psalm 37:3–5)

These verses call upon a person to do things everyone is capable of doing: trust God, praise God, enjoy God's presence, and obey God. The outcomes associated with these things include material provision and protection, emotional well-being, and tremendous success. God will lead us into the paths we should walk and give us the fullness of all that lies along that pathway.

"But," you may be saying, "I don't deserve such goodness. I haven't earned it."

True . . . at least to a degree. You can't earn God's favor. What you can do is receive the gifts that are given out of His loving heart and at His initiative! What you can do is work to the best of your ability, obey God's commandments as fully as you know how, and take delight in all that God gives to you. It is not a matter of earning or deserving, but simply receiving what a loving God has chosen to provide for you.

DELIGHT IN GOD'S GOODNESS TO YOU

I have yet to meet a toddler who doesn't delight in toys. A child may never have seen a toy before, but when handed one, he instantly expresses delight. A parent gives to his child because he loves him, not because the child deserves a toy. A child receives what his parent gives because he delights in receiving, not because he has any sense that he is entitled or that the gift is payment for doing a good job of being a child! Receive from the Lord the spontaneous love gifts that flow from His heart! Give to the Lord the spontaneous love gifts that flow from your heart—your praise, obedience, thanksgiving, service, and presence.

The truth of God's Word is that you are worthy of all the good things God has for you, not because of what you have done, but because of who He is and what Jesus has done on your behalf.

Take a few minutes right now to write down who you are in Christ Jesus. Don't rely solely on what I presented earlier in this chapter. Make your own list! You may need to go to your concordance or consult a friend who is familiar with God's Word. This list may be one of the most valuable things you ever write in your entire life. It is a statement of who you are in God's eyes.

On the basis of who God says you are and what God says you can be, have, and do, begin to believe God with all your heart for everything that He says is best in this life. Ask God to give you a glimpse of where He desires you to contribute or lead and the things He desires to give you so that you might help others. Some of the things God desires to give you are tangible and material. Clip photos of those items and keep them where they are a reminder to you every day. Use those photos to help focus your faith as you ask God to meet your needs, in order that you might fulfill His call on your life.

The Bible tells us to write down what God calls us to do (see Habakkuk 2:2 and Jeremiah 30:2). Collecting photos is a way of writing down the things God desires for you. If God calls you to take in foster children, you will need a home big enough for the children He sends your way. If God calls you to provide transportation for elderly people who no longer can drive themselves to grocery stores or doctors' offices, you will need a car. If God calls you to a foreign missions project for a month, you will need an airline ticket. Get a clear image of precisely what you need in order to fulfill the tasks in front of you.

Remind yourself of how God has provided for you in the past. God's provision in the past is what enabled you to achieve and accomplish what you have done thus far in your life. You didn't earn your current level of success on your own. Other people helped you, and above all, God gave you the health, energy, intelligence, spiritual gifts, scriptural insights, direction, anointing, and opportunities that produced good results and set the stage for the next steps He is calling you to take. The ways God has provided for you, protected you, and poured out His blessings upon you in the past are only the beginning of the ways He desires to do so in the future!

It is very important for you to recognize that if you have ever built or accomplished anything of value or worth in your life, you can do it again and do it better. You simply need to use the same principles, employ the same diligence, and seek to build better next time with the necessary adjustments. It doesn't matter if you've lost the successful business you once built—you can rebuild. It doesn't matter if you were downsized or let go from a job after you had climbed your way to the top of the corporate ladder. Markets change, unforeseen circumstances arise, mistakes are made, catastrophes occur, ownership is transferred, banks stop lending, judgment isn't always perfect. There are any number of reasons beyond a person's control for a venture not to succeed. Furthermore, no person makes it all the way through life without some degree of failure. The point is not whether you will be knocked down by life, but whether you will get up after you are knocked down. Don't get stuck and blame God for what you have lost. Rather, learn from any mistakes you may have made and trust God to help you to do again what He helped you do before.

> No person makes it all the way through life without some degree of failure. The point is not whether you will be knocked down by life, but whether you will get up after you are knocked down.

THANK GOD FOR ALL HE HAS PROVIDED AND DONE

From time to time in the Old Testament, God commanded His people to build small altars or memorials to remember what He had done for them. The memorials or altars were used to sacrifice animals, creatures that God had created, from a flock or herd God had multiplied. A memorial altar, therefore, was a visible sign of a person's thanksgiving and praise to God, who alone supplies all that we need both to build a memorial and to offer a sacrifice. How wonderful for us to remember what God has given to us.

Stop right now and make a list of the things God has given you or done for you in the past.

I don't know what you may have put on your list, but I hope that your memorial list of thanksgivings included items like these:

- People who genuinely love you
- Work that is fulfilling to you
- Personal health and energy and strength—physical, mental, emotional, and spiritual
- Ministry opportunities to bless others
- A safe home
- Friends who are trustworthy, loyal, and helpful, and with whom you can share both your laughter and your tears
- Adequate food, clothing, and shelter
- Finances that are sufficient to do what God has called you to do
- Freedom to speak, think, create, invest, and build
- Freedom to worship and pray and trust God
- Inner peace, fortitude, and vision

Even if you don't have all those things at present, thank God in advance for what you believe He will provide for you! To do this is not an act of presumption or wishful thinking—rather, it's an act of *faith*.

I strongly suggest that you write down five things every day for which you are thankful to God. Just this one simple act can change your perception greatly about who God is and what God desires to do in you, through you, and all around you. You might write these in your journal, or keep a separate running list in a blank book. Any time you become discouraged or frustrated at what you perceive to be a lack of love or opportunity in your life, reread your thanksgiving list. This is strong evidence that God loves you always, in ways great and small.

A PRACTICAL MEANS OF GAINING PERSPECTIVE

One of the best tools that I know for gaining and keeping perspective on your life over time is journaling.

I am a strong advocate of writing in a journal on a regular basis—daily, if possible, but at least weekly. Don't just document what you *do*. It's even more important to write down what you are thinking and feeling, and how you are responding to life around you. Writing your feelings down gives them a sense of validity. After all, they are your feelings, and it is necessary to process them in order for growth to come about. Over time, you'll be able to read back through your journals and see trends. You'll be able to watch how your emotions ebb and flow over time and analyze them more objectively.

I recently read through several of my journals, and I was amazed at how the words I had written on those pages brought up deep emotions. I was struck by the depth of the anguish I had recorded about some of my experiences. Was I embarrassed or dismayed that I had felt such deep pain? Not at all. Rather, I rejoiced that God had brought me through that time victoriously and that He had healed me and strengthened me in very specific ways.

I have long been a believer in the principle that if something doesn't kill you, it makes you stronger, and that if you are able to bend just a little and not break, you can ride out just about any storm. In truth, it is the presence of God in your life that makes you strong and that defeats the enemy that desires to destroy you. It is God who gives you the enduring strength and flexibility to withstand the severest storm in the darkest of nights. Again and again, there are seasons in my life when I cry out to God in my journals, expressing both my pain at the circumstances swirling around me and my deep love for God and joy at His presence.

My journals are private and precious, as I hope your journals are (or will become) to you. They can contribute greatly to your growth and to your sense of balance over the years. They are a reminder that you *always* have great cause to thank and praise God, great evidence for your faith, and great reason for putting all of your trust and dependency upon Him.

BECOME A STUDENT OF YOURSELF

The more you gain a clear perception of who you are in Christ, who God is, and the future that God desires to give you, the clearer your understanding will become about what you are to do day by day. Gaining better insight into your past may very well be the most powerful tool you can have for determining how you will think, speak, and act in your future.

Nobody but God can ever understand you as fully as you can know yourself. I challenge you: discover just how fascinating you are! Nobody has a story quite like yours.

Become an Expert
on the
Subject of You

6

ASK YOURSELF TOUGH "WHY" QUESTIONS

*W*hen something bad happens to us, we are quick to ask, "Why, God? Why me?"

When something good happens to someone else, we are also quick to say, "Why that person, God?" or perhaps, "Why not me?"

God may not always answer the why questions we ask of Him. But He will always help us answer the "why" questions we ask of ourselves. Ask yourself, for example:

- "Why do I keep dealing with these same problems at work—different bosses, different associates, but the same problems?"
- "I've attended five different churches in three years, but I seem to encounter the same problems in each one—why?"
- "Why do I always seem to have trouble with my neighbors, no matter where I live?"
- "Why do I always end up with the same kind of guy—different name, different exterior, but same ol' jerk inside?"

The problems that are at the root of most "why" questions don't primarily exist in other people. They are resident in you and how you perceive yourself.

Take a long look at your own behavior. The Word of God tells us bluntly, "Consider your ways" (Haggai 1:5). It says, "You've sown a lot, but you don't reap much. You eat but aren't filled. You drink but aren't satisfied. You clothe yourself, but you aren't warm. You earn money, but your money bag seems to have holes in it" (Haggai 1:6, paraphrase). In other words, you try and try, but you aren't succeeding. If that's the case in any area of your life, "consider your ways"!

Consider what you are thinking.

Consider what you are saying.

Consider what you are doing.

A deep, introspective consideration of your ways can be painful initially, but in the long run, it will be extremely beneficial. You probably won't like all that you see when you stare long and hard into the depths of your own soul. The good news is that you *can* make the necessary or desirable changes. But you must first be willing to confront yourself.

A man once admitted to me that in the two years since he had moved into his home, he had not been down to the basement of the house. When he did finally descend that staircase, he didn't like what he saw! There was a tremendous sorting, cleaning, and repair job ahead of him. He admitted, "I found evidence of critters—some pests had made their way through a broken window-well screen. I found rust on the water heater that was troublesome. I found debris scattered about, including shreds of clothing and paperwork. The critters had made their way into some boxes of old clothes and paperwork that I had put there when I first moved in. It was a *mess.*"

It took this man four weekends and two trips to the city dump to get his basement into good order. How did he feel once the job was done? "I felt like I'd moved a mountain," he said. "None of the work that I did was evident to any other person in my neighborhood, but I certainly slept better at night knowing that I had a water heater that was reliable and a clean and organized basement that I could actually *use.*" He continued, "And the basement was just the beginning. I decided to take on all the closets in the house after that. Fortunately, there wasn't as big a mess in any of them."

There was a romantic side to his story as well. This story actually arose in conversation because of something his fiancée said. Her answer to the question, "What attracted you to this guy?" was, "He had a clean basement." And why was that attractive? She replied, "I knew that a man who cared enough to have a clean basement, which nobody sees, is a person who would deal with his own messes and who wouldn't try to hide things just to save face. I figured what was evident on the outside was a good sign of what was on the inside. He was a man who had good values and would be honest in telling me what he was feeling and thinking, and honest in telling me what he believed."

She was right!

Cleaning out, sorting, or repairing the damage in your inner self is very much like cleaning out a damaged basement. It's hard work. Nobody else may see or appreciate what you are doing. But it's hugely beneficial, and ultimately will make you far more attractive to others.

SORT OUT YOUR TWO NATURES

All of us have two people inside us—a "flesh" side and a "God" side. One of Jesus's followers, a man we know as Simon Peter, is a clear example of this. The name Simon refers to a reed. *Simon* was this man's weak and wavering side. *Peter* is a name that means "rock"—it refers to strength and stability.

At one point Jesus said to him, "But I have prayed for you, Simon, that your faith may not fail" (Luke 22:32 NIV). Jesus addressed the human, fleshly, flaky side of Simon Peter. Jesus could foresee the day in the not-too-distant future when Peter would stand strong and preach a sermon after which thousands of people would accept Jesus as the Christ. But at the time of Jesus's prayer, He was praying for the fleshly part of Simon Peter.

God sees your future. He knows the beginning and the end of your life, and He knows that you will walk into that future with confidence and faith only if you confront and deal with the weak and wavering side of who you are today.

Every man has a Superman side and a Clark Kent side. Every woman has a Superwoman side and a girl-next-door side. The positive "super-person" part of you can develop, grow, and prevail. But know that before that can happen fully, you need to deal with the negative or weaker part of you.

> The positive "super-person" part of you can develop, grow, and prevail.

The apostle Peter had tremendous leadership potential, strong faith, a willingness to take risks with his faith, and an ability to make deep, heartfelt commitments. But Peter was also capable of denying Jesus three times, and of erupting in anger to the point of using a sword to cut off a servant's ear. Peter had to gain control of the Simon part of his personality before he could experience the fullness of God's call on his life.

To walk into the fullness of who you can be—the person God created you to be—you must first deal with those things that are holding you back from your own potential. What are some of those things?

Some of them may be externals.

You may need more education or training.

You may need better manners.

You may need to get out and meet new people and develop better social skills.

All of these externals, however, begin on the inside, with a firm awareness of who you are.

You *can* learn and develop new skills, and you *should*, because you are intelligent and capable.

You *can* and *should* acquire better manners in order to move freely in society, because you are worthy of being fully accepted any place you go.

You *can* and *should* get out and meet new people, because they should get to know the wonderful person you are.

I once met a woman who had been disappointed in love and who had refused to date for a couple of years. She said, "I was scared of dating.

It never worked for me. I decided I'd rather stay home and watch TV." Well, not only did she stay home and watch too much television, but she snacked too much while doing so. One day she took a long "consider your ways" look in the mirror and said, "This isn't the real me." She started walking and dieting and lost forty pounds.

While walking in the park one day, she noticed that there was a man walking about the same time of day that she walked. Over the weeks and months, he also lost weight. She commented on that fact one day, while they were both resting by a drinking fountain after their walks. He complimented her in return. They began to talk about where they lived and where they worked, and that conversation led to a decision to meet for lunch. You get the picture . . . and the story did have a happy ending! They fell in love and were married.

But what if she had refused to have her "consider your ways" moment? Without that confrontation, there would never have been the action that led her to achievements and satisfaction.

MAKE AN OBJECTIVE APPRAISAL OF YOURSELF

To be objective is to focus on facts, not opinions or feelings. An objective appraisal is free of bias and prejudice. It is what would stand up in a court of law, totally independent of your thoughts, perceptions, or even input.

Having an objective view of yourself can be difficult. The key is to focus solely on facts. Take a look at your history, your accomplishments, and your abilities. Deal with what *is*, not what you'd like or what you desire. Work hard to identify your strengths and the positive attributes of your life. Most people find it easier to see their flaws than their strengths, but in truth, we all have strengths that need to be brought to the forefront of our thinking.

What are some of the things you should consider as part of taking an objective view of yourself? I've listed twenty-five categories below, and I've put a question or two for you to ask about each of these. Take some time with this objective appraisal of yourself. Be as thorough as possible. I believe you'll find the experience rewarding.

AN OBJECTIVE APPRAISAL OF SELF

AREA FOR APPRAISAL	QUESTIONS TO ASK
1. Spiritual health	What are my spiritual gifts? What is my spiritual state? Do I have a relationship with God through His Son, Jesus? Who am I in Christ?
2. Emotional health	How stable am I emotionally? How well do I handle change or crises? Can I properly identify and address my emotions?
3. Physical health	How healthy am I? What are my physical traits? What are my physical strengths? Do I value my health as a gift and respect it by properly caring for it?
4. Financial health	What is my financial status? Debt? Income? How much of my earnings do I save? How much of my earnings do I contribute to church or charitable causes?
5. Commitments	To whom am I committed and in what ways? Is that in alignment with the authentic me? Am I responsible with the commitments I have made?
6. Value system	What are my values? What won't I do? How do I decide what to do?
7. Family	Who are my close family members? What is the nature of our relationship? Am I satisfied with the function of that relationship?
8. Friends	Who are my friends? What is the nature of our relationship? What do I provide as a friend?
9. Life interests	What am I most interested in doing or accomplishing in my life? What do I still desire to learn or experience?
10. Goals	What do I desire to achieve? What do I want to leave behind as a legacy? How do I want to be remembered in history? How do I want to be acknowledged by God in Heaven?

AREA FOR APPRAISAL	QUESTIONS TO ASK
11. Violations	What has been done to me in the past that should not have been done to me? What have I done to others that I should not have done? Are there consequences I'm still facing because of these violations?
12. Trust	Who do I trust? How quickly do I trust? What does it take for me to trust? What does trust mean to me?
13. Communication	How good am I at communicating verbally? In writing? How good am I at listening? How can I improve my communication skills?
14. Children	How do I relate to the children in my life? What do I hope for them? How close am I to each of them? Do I see their value and giftings in life and nurture those? What is my spiritual relationship with each of them? (If you do not have children of your own, consider your spiritual children or beloved children—including nieces, nephews, or godchildren.)
15. Ministry	What has God put in my heart to do to win lost souls? What do I desire to do to benefit my fellow Christians and to serve hurting humanity? How prepared am I for the ministry I believe I am to have?
16. Protection and safety issues	How safe and secure do I believe I am? Where are areas of weakness?
17. Cares and concerns	What concerns me most? What do I really care about? What injustice do I desire to see brought to justice? What hurt or ill in the world do I long to see healed or resolved?
18. Nurture	Who looks to me to provide nurture—care, attention, affection, provision, protection? Who nurtures me? Do I feel satisfied with the amount of nurturing I give and receive?

AREA FOR APPRAISAL	QUESTIONS TO ASK
19. Flexibility and ability to make transitions	How flexible am I? How quickly can I adapt to new situations or circumstances? How comfortable am I with change? How quickly do I respond to a crisis or challenge?
20. Support	Who provides support to me? Who can I count on? Who do I rely upon to tell me the truth, give me accurate factual information or an honest opinion?
21. Honor	What or who do I honor? Who are my role models? What honors or recognitions have I been given? Who looks to me as a role model?
22. Needs	What are the foremost needs in my life (including material, emotional, spiritual)? How do I usually go about getting my needs met? What needs have been met in the past that I consider to have been "major" needs? Where do I turn for help in meeting my needs?
23. Knowledge	How have I intentionally developed my mental capacity? In what am I an "expert"? What has been the focus of my formal study? What do I want to learn in the coming year? Where can I get the information or instruction I desire?
24. Time	How do I budget my time in any given day or week? In what areas do I tend to allot too little or too much time?
25. Respect	Who do I respect? How do I show respect? Do I feel respected? In what ways?

We'll explore a few of these areas in greater depth in the pages ahead, but one of the issues that you need to deal with at a foundational level before we proceed is this: do I esteem myself in a healthy way?

EVALUATE ISSUES RELATED TO YOUR SELF-ESTEEM

A number of scientific research studies have shown that the two greatest factors for overall life satisfaction are confidence and healthy self-esteem.

I define self-esteem as a "realistic appreciative opinion of self." *Realistic* means that the person is objective and honest. *Appreciative* means positive. In other words, for you to have good self-esteem means that you hold an honest, positive view of yourself.

This does not mean that you are in denial about your faults or that you don't see any areas for improvement. Rather, it means that you are able to see your strengths and that you believe you are capable of improving, growing, and developing. Even when you know that you have "rough edges," you like who you are and believe that you have value.

Take stock of your self-esteem level. Identify the degree to which you agree with each of the statements below.

SELF-ESTEEM EVALUATION

	LOW AGREEMENT	MEDIUM AGREEMENT	HIGH AGREEMENT
I'm a valuable person.			
I have good qualities.			
I can laugh at myself.			
I deserve to be appreciated.			

	LOW AGREEMENT	MEDIUM AGREEMENT	HIGH AGREEMENT
I am worthy of respect from others.			
I feel confident.			
I feel free to be me.			
I like myself.			
I have undeniable dignity.			
I'm satisfied with the person I've become.			
I respect myself.			
I'd rather be me than anybody else.			
I reward myself in positive ways.			
I enjoy being alone.			

	LOW AGREEMENT	MEDIUM AGREEMENT	HIGH AGREEMENT
I feel good about myself.			
I think highly of myself.			

Take a look at the pattern of your responses. Are they on the "low agreement" side of the scale or the "high agreement" side of the scale?

High, positive self-esteem is very closely linked to self-appreciation. Do not dismiss the tremendous value that lies in loving and appreciating yourself. Jesus taught His followers that they were to love others *as they loved themselves* (see Matthew 22:39).

Unconditional means absolute, having no limits or restrictions, unqualified. It's a sad fact that we all want unconditional love, but we rarely love ourselves unconditionally.

LOVE YOURSELF UNCONDITIONALLY

Unconditional love is a concept that we hear about, and most of us desire to receive unconditional love. It's a tremendous benefit to know that God gives us unconditional love. To give unconditional love is not easy. It certainly isn't automatic. To love unconditionally is to love someone solely because they exist. If you attach any form of behavior, any form of exchange or mutuality, or any form of accomplishment or performance to love, then your love becomes "conditional." For many people, the only truly unconditional love they give is to a child. Good parents love their children solely because those children exist on this earth. Even in the best of marriages, conditional lines tend to exist. Just ask yourself, "What wouldn't I ever put up with?" and you'll find yourself very close to establishing a condition.

The one person that most people never think of loving unconditionally is themselves! This type of love is essential, however, if you are truly to live an authentic life.

Do you genuinely appreciate yourself, for no other reason than the fact that you are alive?

Do you value your personhood—your life, your potential, your dreams, your talents?

Do you take care of yourself, doing your best to nurture and nourish yourself? To nourish yourself is to take in the best "nutrients," not only for your body, but for your mind, emotions, and spirit. To nurture yourself is to get sufficient rest and time for contemplation and reflection—not only sleep for your body, but genuine rest for your mind and heart. To nurture yourself is to take a day a week to put your focus on spiritual renewal, spending time with God and with family and friends who will join you in praising, thanking, and worshiping God. Taking care of yourself means pursuing the highest level of health you can achieve. It means setting goals for your personal benefit, and not feeling guilty as you pursue those goals.

> You can't give anything of benefit to another person unless you first possess it yourself.

Does this sound selfish to you? The truth is that you can't begin to give out to others unless you have something to give! The quality of your giving is directly related to the way in which you unconditionally love yourself.

You can't forgive unless you first receive God's forgiveness and forgive yourself.

You can't live without judging or condemning, unless you first receive God's mercy and stop being so harsh and stop punishing yourself.

You can't give unless you first have a reservoir of love inside you.

You can't give anything of benefit to another person unless you first possess it yourself. You can't give what you don't have.

The positive side of this is extremely encouraging: when you do have something inside you to give, giving is not a chore! Loving and forgiving are immediate, spontaneous, generous, and easy. The loving and giving just spontaneously flow out of you like a bubbling artesian well.

A HEALTHY EQ

Self-esteem is also directly linked to a person's "emotional intelligence quotient," which is a concept similar to a person's "intelligence quotient," or IQ. A person's EQ helps predict how well that person can manage and maximize positive emotional energy, engage fully in life, and develop good relationships that are marked by mutual sharing and trust. The ability to enjoy life is also a factor of EQ.

Nobody can audit your EQ as well as you can.

How frequently do you have a sense of joy? Rarely, sometimes, or often?

How frequently do you have a sense of fulfillment? Rarely, sometimes, or often?

How frequently do you have a deep sense of satisfaction? Rarely, sometimes, or often?

If you rarely have feelings of joy, fulfillment, and deep satisfaction, you are low on the EQ scale. The person with low EQ tends to be impatient, low in confidence, closed to other people, and may struggle when it comes to controlling impulses or handling temptation. In all likelihood, you are not maximizing energy in your life, and you are likely low in patience, self-confidence, and openness to others. You probably struggle to control impulses in your life, frequently give in to temptation, and have very little empathy for others. You may struggle to trust others and enjoy life, and you probably aren't very effective in your personal relationships. The good news is that you can begin to transform today and see those depleted areas filled and restored.

Those who frequently feel joy, and have an abiding sense of fulfillment and deep satisfaction, are people who are very likely high in emotional energy. They tend to be people who are patient, self-confident, and open to others. They are in control of their behavior, empathetic, and able to trust others and enjoy life. They have relationships that are interdependent—with mutual giving and receiving.

The lower your EQ, the more you need to get away from the pressure cooker of life and take time to process what you are feeling. The lower your EQ, the more you need to make a serious evaluation of yourself and gain an understanding of why you respond to things the way you do. You owe it to yourself as a valuable vessel of this gift called life.

EVALUATE YOUR POTENTIAL FOR MINISTRY

The Bible challenges those who believe in God to make themselves "living sacrifices"—fully giving themselves to serving God and other people (see Romans 12:1). Before you seek to help another person, you need to see yourself as having something to give! That's what "ministry" is. It isn't necessarily a full-time job as a pastor or evangelist or counselor. Ministry is what you give to bless another person.

People who have a faulty self-perception that produces low self-worth are often very guarded in what they say and do because they don't want to be used, abused, or taken advantage of. The truth is, every person who has been forgiven of her past and has a good relationship with God has a tremendous amount to give. Such a person is fully equipped to give hope to other people. Take the attitude that if God can forgive you, He can forgive anybody!

All of us come to God desperately in need of the forgiveness He bestows. And the greatest news any person can ever hear is that God does fully forgive. In fact, the Bible says that whoever comes to God admitting she needs forgiveness is a person who God freely and completely forgives (see 1 John 1:9).

You can know God's forgiveness. And once you have experienced God's forgiveness, there's nothing holding you back from sharing that good news with other people.

I once heard about a young woman who had come out of the hippie drugs-and-free-sex culture of the 1960s. She had used drugs and had had a couple of abortions. Then she heard about God's forgiveness and accepted it for her life. She became part of a church, and after she had been at the church about six months, the pastor realized that *most* of the new members in the last few months had joined the church because of her. He said to her, "You are one of the best recruiters this church has ever known. What is it that you say to people?"

She said, "Not much, really. I just tell people, 'I was really messed up and Jesus cleaned me up. He forgave me and gave me a brand new start. Isn't that great?' Nobody has ever argued with me. And some of the people I've told have asked me, 'Do you think Jesus can give anybody a brand new start?' I tell them yes and invite them to meet me at church on Sunday."

This woman had a twenty-three-word message to give to people. She didn't quote the Bible or offer deep theological answers. She didn't go on and on about how badly she had been messed up. She cut to the chase with good news. And dozens of people experienced God's forgiveness as a result.

When people see how God turned your failures into successes, your "messed up" state into a "cleaned up" state, and your past into your future, they will want to know more about how God can work in their lives. The point is never how bad you were or how good you've become, but rather the truth that you have been and are being transformed by God into someone new, better, purer, and free. That transforming process is promised to every person who accepts God into her life.

Stop seeing yourself as a person with a past. See yourself as someone who is being transformed. The best part of your life has yet to be lived!

Stop seeing yourself as limited by what you have experienced. See yourself as having an experience with God that He can use to bless someone else.

Stop seeing yourself as being stuck in an unforgiven, messed-up state. Accept God's forgiveness and allow Him to work inside you to change you from the inside-out into the person He designed you to be.

FRAME "WHY" ANSWERS

Knowing who you are can help you answer the tough "why" questions about your past behavior and future expectations. Developing a clear perception of yourself can reveal many of the causes for the effects of your life. Now let's move on to even deeper ways to know the authentic you—and to set yourself free!

7

FOUR CRITICAL INSIGHTS

*A*s you become an expert on your core identity, there are several areas I strongly encourage you to probe patiently and fully. Gaining understanding in these areas will make all the difference in living an authentic life—one that brings the maximum satisfaction and produces the greatest legacy.

KNOW THE SEASON AND LIFESPAN YOU ARE IN

I have learned two great lessons from a gardener friend. One of them is that some plants are annuals (yearly, one-time bloom), others are perennials (last beyond a year; several or many blooms). It's important to know the difference. If you spend a great deal of time and energy trying to get an annual plant to live beyond its life span, you will likely be very frustrated and disappointed. Know what you are dealing with! Some projects, some results, some jobs, and some relationships are for the short-term of your life, others are for longer seasons, and some are even for eternity.

Know what season you are in. This simple principle applies to both relationships and tasks. Some things in your life may need to be jettisoned. When a space shuttle takes off, all rockets are fired and the force is tremendous. A few minutes later, booster rockets are fired to take the shuttle into outer space. Once these launch-related rockets have been fired, they are jettisoned away from the aircraft. Their purpose has been fulfilled.

Some of the things that God allows into your life are for a short-term launch to propel you into new levels of information, skill, or understanding. God doesn't intend those experiences, jobs, or mentors to be with you always—in fact, they can become dead weight to you if you try to hold on to them. Learn what it is that you are to learn, acquire the skills you are to acquire, experience what God has for you to experience, and then be willing to let go. God has exciting plans for the next season of your life.

I certainly am not negating the fact that God does intend for some relationships to be "perennial." Marriage is intended for the long haul of life. We don't jettison our children or grandchildren or other family members. We nurture and develop some friendships so that they become lifelong friendships. Other relationships, however, may have limits to them. Ask God what He wants you to release from your life.

Is it time to quit that club? To give up that membership?

Is it time to release a relationship that is spiritually or emotionally harmful?

Is it time to move from that neighborhood?

If there are people in your life who routinely trample the Word of God, jettison them from your life. I don't care if Lou Ann and Tamika and Carmen and Lotus have been your friends for decades; if they are intent upon stealing the Word of God from your heart or influencing you to spend less time in the presence of God, they need to be removed from your life. Don't be rude or mean in breaking off your association with these doubters. Simply say "No, thank you" to their invitations.

Invest your time and energy in relationships that are perennial and eternal.

The story is told of a father who spent an entire day working with his young son on a bicycle—repairing the broken chain and the banged-up frame, oiling the chain and cleaning the bike, adding a mirror and putting on new handlebar grips. A neighbor watched the all-day effort, and in the evening, came across the street to talk to the father. "Why didn't you just take the bike to the bicycle shop and have it repaired?" he asked the father. "It could have been done in just an hour, and you could certainly afford the repair."

The father replied, "I wasn't just fixing a bike today. I was building a son."

Spend time building relationships. Choose a task that is beneficial to somebody. Enjoy the process of working on the task together, talking and sharing, in order to build each other up emotionally, mentally, and spiritually.

How do we build up other people in a task-oriented process?

Offer encouragement and praise for the work they do.

Share the stories of your life that can inspire them to face their own difficult challenges with courage and joy.

Talk about noble ideas, truths that are eternal, and goals that are worth pursuing.

See beyond the external layers of their lives into the beauty of their souls, and help them identify, nurture, and release the greatness they have on the inside.

KNOW THE SEASON OF YOUR LIFE

Overall, life tends to have seasons. Evaluate which season you may be in, and recognize that *all* seasons have a purpose.

Winter. Winter is the time to reflect by the fireplace, rest, and allow your body to be restored and your mind and emotions to be healed. Don't allow yourself to be discouraged. Don't let "gray days" overwhelm you. Don't focus on what was in the past, and don't daydream too much about the spring ahead. Eventually, the winter season ends. Use it for good while it lasts.

Early winter is a great time for pruning so that the growth of spring will be maximized. Winter is the time to plan the spring garden and to prepare all things necessary for planting it. It's the time for preparing the soil and removing dead brush. Use this wintertime in your life for inner work. Explore what God desires to teach you and how God desires to prepare you for the season ahead.

Spring. This season is one of renewal and growth. Life flourishes. New things are started. This is a time for output and fresh new ventures. It isn't enough just to *plan* a garden—you must actually *plant* a garden if you want vegetables or flowers. Consult with others who are experiencing the kind of harvest you one day hope to experience. Discover how they began their career or ministry. Take advantage of their wisdom and learn from them more about what works and what doesn't work. Then take the beginning steps necessary for turning your dream into a reality.

Summer. Summer days can seem long and hot, but this is the season for work and more work. It is the season for plowing and cultivating and irrigating. The work can seem tedious at times, but it's work that needs to be done. Don't give up. Keep doing the good that you know to do. Hang in there until the project is complete. If you are a parent, you may have to remind yourself to be patient until the child moves through a particular phase of her life. If you are in the middle of a campaign or long-term program, persevere in maintaining your momentum and in doing what you know is right before God.

Autumn. The harvest does eventually come (see Galatians 6:7–10). Autumn is the time for rejoicing in your fruitfulness, for reaping rewards, and for sharing God's goodness with family and friends.

Ask God to reveal what season you are in right now.

The external seasons of our lives are more obvious than internal ones. A sixty-year-old woman trying to wear the miniskirt fashions of the teen-agers is out of her season. So is the twelve-year-old carrying a briefcase and wearing high heels and too much makeup.

Internally, we sometimes cling to old routines, old habits, or old ways of thinking. Old associations that are no longer relevant to our lives or important to our purpose. Go to God and ask, "What season am I in when it comes to this project, this affiliation, this membership, this task, this relationship?"

As a part of identifying the seasons of life, keep in mind this principle: all situations are temporary. Life is a process. Don't become discouraged with the season you are in. Don't take for granted the season you are sovereignly assigned to. Learn to enjoy the beauty of each moment. Trust God to bring your life to a "happy ending."

KNOW THE UNIQUE CHARACTERISTICS OF WHAT GOD IS GROWING IN YOU

My gardener friend also taught me that not all plants need the same amount of sunlight, water, and fertilizer. My friend once put a purple-leafed houseplant in a sunny window and watered and fertilized it often, but to his surprise, the plant withered and started to die. When he went to the garden center where he had purchased the plant and asked for their advice, he learned that this particular plant thrives in dim light, with much less water than most plants.

Some people live through the most horrendous circumstances and emerge strong. God uses very difficult situations to make and mold them into the people He desires for them to be. I often say, "If it didn't kill you, it made you stronger." Many people I know today have survived what easily could have killed them. They have been through agonizing, horrific experiences. But the greater truth of their lives is that God was with them in those terrifying, terrible traumas, and His presence empowered them in such a way that they are far stronger today than they ever thought they could be. God does not send situations into our lives to crush us, but rather to refine us, so that we can be of great use and help to both ourselves and others.

The more you discover your own unique characteristics, the more you are likely to develop a tolerance and empathy for the unique characteristics of others. God does not work in the same way with all people, all the time. His principles are true and fixed, but his methods are as varied as there are people on the earth.

RECOGNIZE THAT GOD USES DIFFERENT METHODS TO SHAPE US

This is such a vital lesson! We often think that God works solely in the way we have experienced His presence and power in our lives. But the fact is that God is multi-faceted. As one person said to me, "There is often more than one path to the top of the mountain."

God's principles and the role of Jesus Christ, His Son, are fixed. God's methods for bringing a person to accept forgiveness through Jesus as Savior are *many*. God's plan varies for each of us.

Ask God if there is a better way for you to live. Is there a better means for accomplishing His goals for your life?

Ask God to show you what you can learn from the situation in which you find yourself. Ask, "Why do I do this in this particular way? Is it Your way, God?" "Why have I made this a habit in my life?" "What does this mean for my future?"

Many good habits and routines are worth keeping! Don't discard them. Other habits and routines are a waste of your time; their purpose in your life has come and gone. Some experiences that you regard as failures are actually experiences that hold great lessons for you. Learn the lessons before moving on.

I learned a couple of those lessons early in my preaching ministry. I was invited to a particular church to speak and, as is my normal custom, I spent long hours preparing the sermon that I believed God wanted me to preach. I went to the church, and I was committed to preaching that sermon exactly as I had prepared it. My message, however, was not a relevant one to the congregation before me. I had done good research into God's Word, but I hadn't done enough research about the people who were going to be present. I had the right message, but not in the right place to the right people.

Furthermore, there were logistical problems that day, so the service was running way behind schedule. I had originally been told I would start preaching at 9:30 in the morning, and have two hours. Well, I wasn't able to start until 11:30, but I was determined to get my full message preached. Eleven thirty in the morning is *not* the time to begin a long, build-from-the-ground-to-the-sky sermon!

And there's still more. The air conditioning in the building quit working that morning. The room was at least fifteen degrees hotter than it should have been. I was miserable. The people were miserable. But I was determined to preach my full message.

The result? A big disappointment. A disaster.

I was embarrassed as I sat alone in my room after that experience. I quickly crumpled up my sermon notes and complained to God, "I thought I was called. How could You let that happen to me?"

Then I asked the more important question, "What really happened here, Paula?" I quickly realized that I could learn some important lessons from that experience. I needed to do more thorough research into what the congregation's needs were. My sermon was a good sermon—it just wasn't for those people. And I needed to not be afraid to shorten the message or adapt it to the environment. I knew the Word but had not been seasoned to effectively deliver what God had given me for His people. Those lessons have been invaluable to me in the years since that experience. But it took a failure—or should I say a *few* failures?—for me to learn them.

What does God desire to teach you? How does He desire to use the current situation in your life to shape you for what He has ahead for you?

KNOW GOOD CHARACTER FROM BAD CHARACTER

Character reveals who a person is. One person's nature can't be changed by another person. That's a key fact you must face. Only God can change a person's nature. Don't think that you will be the cause of reform or definitive healing of another person's psychosis, neurosis, or any other form of emotional or mental disorder or instability. Don't think you can be another person's savior or deliverer—that's the exclusive work of God.

Don't expect anybody else to "fix" your character. Your pastor can't do it. Your spouse can't do it. Only God can mold your character.

LEARN WHAT IT MEANS TO HAVE GOOD CHARACTER

Two experiences early in my life gave me important clues about character. The first experience occurred before I was a teenager. I found an envelope on the floor of the commissary (a military grocery store) and when I picked it up and looked inside, I discovered the envelope had $2,500 in it. My stepfather was a military man, and I knew that $2,500 was significant for

any military person or family. I knew immediately that this envelope probably held all the money a family needed to live for an entire pay period.

There was never any question in my mind or heart—I had to go
immediately to the store manager and turn in the envelope. Sure enough,
as soon as an announcement was made over the public-address system
in the store, a woman came forward to claim the money. She was overwhelmed with emotion, to the point of having tears in her eyes, but I
don't think it ever dawned on her to offer me any reward for turning in
the envelope. And that was okay. I learned that day that it didn't really
matter if I got a reward for doing the right thing; the greatest satisfaction
is knowing within myself that I've done the right thing.

The second big character lesson I learned early in my life happened one
night when I was sixteen years old. I was working a late shift at a fast-food
restaurant. I always worked hard, and still do. I'm not afraid of long hours
or extra effort. I liked the closing shift at this establishment, even though it
meant the extra effort of cleaning out various food bins and machines.

Virtually all of the people who worked with me on that shift gave away
food to family members and friends who came by. It was easy to see how they
justified their behavior. After all, if the salad bar or milkshake machine had to
be cleaned out and all the food tossed in an hour or so, why not give some of
that to a hungry husband or child? I watched everybody around me break the
rules, but something inside me said, "That isn't right for you. Don't do it."

Then one night, my boyfriend came in a little while before closing and
ordered some French fries and something to drink. When he got out his
money to pay, I said, "Never mind about that," and waved him away from
the counter so I could wait on the next person. Who, it turned out, was the
district manager of the fast-food chain. At the close of that shift, I was fired.

Did I argue with the decision? No.

Did I try to justify my behavior? No.

I didn't even plead for mercy. I knew I hadn't done what was right.
And the lesson I walked away with that night was this: I must always do
what is right within myself, regardless of what other people do. It's what
I call PI, Personal Integrity. It is the value system we set within ourselves
and live by every day.

God *always* sees what we do. Our character is what we do in the dark, even if nobody but God sees our thoughts, words, or actions. Character is what you do instinctively and consistently.

The Bible says that the person with good character will instinctively, habitually do what is loving, what brings joy and peace to her own heart and to others, what reflects patience, what is kind and merciful and forgiving, and what has the hallmarks of discipline and self-control (see Galatians 5:22–23).

We know honesty from dishonesty.

We know truth from lies.

We know greed from generosity.

We know when we are being conned, manipulated, controlled, or brainwashed—at least in most cases.

At times, we can be lulled into justifying behavior that contradicts our true character, or we can even develop a tolerance for that behavior. But in the end, unless our conscience has been completely seared by repeated willful wrong choices, we know deep within our spirit when something feels right and when it feels wrong.

Ask yourself, "What do I do that I intuitively sense deep within me is wrong or misses the mark? What choices and behavior prevent me from living the abundant life God has designed for me?" That's an area for change!

STUDY THE CHARACTER OF OTHERS

Some months ago, I was in my study working hard on next Sunday's sermon, and I had a nagging feeling that something wasn't quite right—not with the sermon, but with me. I finally focused on myself long enough to realize that my feet were aching, and even though I was sitting in a comfortable chair and wasn't wearing any shoes, the ache was persistent. Because my feet hurt, all of me hurt.

How did I end up with such aching feet? Well . . . there had been these extremely cute shoes in the store window with very high heels, and before I knew it, I was walking out of the store with the shoes in a box. The store didn't have my size, but they had a pair a size too small, and—you guessed it—I wore those too-small, way-high, extremely cute shoes out to dinner. Here I was, overriding principles that I had learned to live by as if there would be no cause and effect. Inwardly, I knew not to get those shoes . . . but they were just so cute! Have you ever found yourself caught between desire and obedience when the two do not match up? I ignored the pain that night, but the pain would not let me ignore it for the next several days. I ached all over because I disregarded the better choice and tried to force something that didn't fit me!

Was I stupid to do that? Yes.

Did I ignore logic and reason to get what I wanted? Yes.

Did I pay dearly for those bad choices? Yes!

How many people end up in pain because of their own poor choices, choices they knew were unwise? Choices that they knew, deep on the inside, did not fit them?

She was just so beautiful. I dismissed the fact that she didn't get along with *anyone*.

He was just so charming. I ignored the fact that he drove a fancy car and had nice clothes but couldn't tell me where he worked.

She was so complimentary and supportive of everything I said and did. I chose to run right past the fact that she was complimenting even my mistakes and flaws.

He was just so generous. I overlooked the fact that he hung out with volatile people in dark environments.

Honestly evaluate the values another person holds. How can you tell? By the fruit in their lives.

If Larry has had thirty jobs in the last ten years and is talking about quitting his current job because he has to be there so early in the morning, face up to the fact that he is lazy.

If Olivia has a new outfit on every time you see her but works at a minimum wage job, face up to the fact that she is likely overspending and she may be in serious credit card debt.

If Phil has had four children by four different women and hasn't married any of them, face up to the fact that he is philandering. He probably won't be faithful to you or marry you, but he may try to get you pregnant.

Study *why* a person does what he does. Dig deep. This is not so you can be judgmental—that should be left in the hands of God, who knows all things, including motives. This is for you to be realistic in understanding the role of each relationship in your life. The more you understand and can evaluate character, the easier you will find it to begin healthy relationships and end unhealthy ones. Trust me on this: it's far better to have a *short* bad relationship than a *long* bad relationship.

You cannot and will not change a person permanently. Therefore, evaluate the depth, dimension, and purpose of your relationship honestly and objectively. Ask yourself, "Why do I attract people with certain behaviors or qualities into my life?" It is only when you discover the answers to these questions that you can develop the healthy, whole, and satisfying relationships you desire. I often say that you don't go to the shoe store to buy bananas. What do I mean by that? You're looking in the wrong place for what you want. Know what you are looking for and where you are likely to find it.

KNOW WHERE YOU ARE GOING AND WHY

There's an old saying, "Are you just traveling? Or are you going somewhere?" Many people get caught up in the busyness of life. They think that because they are moving at a breakneck speed eighteen hours a day, they *should* reach success—ideally, sooner rather than later. The truth is, just being busy doesn't produce results. Pause for a moment and take stock of what you are doing and why.

I've talked to dozens upon dozens of people about this through the years, and it's very rare that I find a person who ever questions, "Why am I doing all that I'm doing?"

> Line up every activity and habit in every day with your broader purposes and goals.

Take a full inventory of all that you do and ask, "Why?" Much of what you do may be necessary or important. Chances are, however, that you'll discover some things that are neither necessary nor important. Jettison those things!

Make it your goal to have everything in your life pointed toward the same direction and the same results. Line up every activity and habit in every day with your broader purposes and goals.

THE RIGHT AMOUNT OF RIGHT THINGS

Too much of even the best things can be a bad thing. We certainly know this when it comes to food. The same holds true, however, for the commitments we make. All commitments take emotional energy. All obligations take time and effort. Know your own limitations when it comes to time, skill, and emotional energy.

Is there something in your life that you are overdoing? It may be something good! Many people feel overly responsible for the care they give. Many spend too many hours at work or in ministry, to the neglect of their families or their own personal health and well-being. Output always needs to be balanced with input.

The Word of God has a story about a woman named Dorcas who did very good things in her life—but she died in the course of doing them (see Acts 9:36–37). The apostle Peter came to her and raised her from the dead, but as part of that miracle, he first put out all of the other people from the room where the body of Dorcas lay. Other people may very well have been part of the equation that killed Dorcas. If so, then those other people needed to be removed from the equation for Dorcas to live again.

That may be the case in your life. There may be some obligations you need to give up—even though they are very "good" things—in order to live and not die. If the demand is greater than the supply, even good works and good people can bring some kind of death to your life.

The more clearly you identify your goals and direction in life, the easier it will be for you to evaluate whether something or someone is good or bad for you, whether it is appropriate to the season you are in, and whether your efforts to achieve the greater goals of your life are being helped or hindered.

8

CONDUCT YOUR OWN
NEEDS ANALYSIS

A major planning tool in businesses, school systems, and churches in recent years is a "needs analysis," in which organizational leaders ask themselves to determine what their groups truly need, and use the answers to better analyze what they might do to maximize available resources for optimal results.

I'm all for doing a personal needs analysis for the very same reasons. When you know what you really need, you have a strong mandate for what you must do.

Certainly we all have the same basic needs for air, water, food, and shelter. We need clothing and transportation. We have a spiritual need to connect with God. (Even people who deny that God exists often spend a great deal of time and effort trying to convince themselves of their position, and in a rather skewed way, these efforts "connect" them to God!)

People everywhere are motivated by the same basic emotional needs. We each have a need to:

- Feel worthy, important, significant
- Experience a degree of emotional stability and security

- Learn, take on challenges, and grow
- Receive love, affirmation, and recognition
- Make a contribution and connect with others

It is extremely important that you recognize these basic needs. They are very likely the forces motivating you toward establishing every relationship in your life that you perceive will be long-lasting and fulfilling. As you establish a foundation from basic needs, you will then begin to add specific needs to your individual life.

TAKE A CLOSER LOOK AT YOUR NEED FOR LOVE

At the root of all emotional needs is the need for love. God created you with that need, and He alone is capable of providing the deepest love to fill your deepest need.

When a person doesn't feel loved, she has a very deep and abiding uneasiness—anxiety, fear, churning restlessness. The human heart continually seeks the love it craves, often looking in all the wrong places and in all the wrong ways. People often believe that if they "are just good enough," "do enough," or "acquire enough," they will be lovable; they will have value; their lives will have meaning and significance. The truth of God's Word is that you are loved solely because you are God's creation.

God's Word says that God alone is capable of loving with a perfect love that drives out all fear and anxiety and replaces it with an abiding peace (see 1 John 4:18).

THE NATURE OF GOD'S LOVE

The Bible tells us that God's nature is love (see 1 John 4:16). Because God is unceasingly forgiving, his love "covers a multitude of sins" (see 1 Peter 4:8). Because God is all-powerful, all-knowing, and eternal, his love is unconditional—nothing can keep Him from loving. No other person or power, no situation or circumstance, can cause God to stop loving.

Because God is perfect, His love is the purest, most sublime form of love we can ever experience.

Our hearts desire love that is true and authentic. God alone has an unlimited supply of true, authentic love to pour into our innermost being (see 1 John 4:16–18).

Furthermore, the Word of God tells us that God is continually reaching out to us with His love, wooing us to Himself (see 1 John 4:19). God loved us long before we were lovable! He loved us when we were a mess. He loved us at our worst (see Romans 5:8).

This is an almost incomprehensible, unfathomable thought to many people. I have seen the look in the eyes of more people than I can count: "God loved me when I was at my lowest point, engaging in the worst sins, and denying His existence?" The answer is a resounding, joyful "Yes!"

"But why?" you may ask. "Why would God love me in that state?"

God loves you because He made you. He fashioned everything about you (see Psalm 139:13–18). He gave you your personality, your talents and abilities, your opportunities, your mind and intelligence, your heart and emotions, your dreams and creativity. He gave you every bit of strength and energy you have. He gives you air for every breath He causes your lungs to breathe. He gives you your every heartbeat.

God loves who you are and who He created you to be. He loves you because you are His craftsmanship, His "creation."

You were designed by a loving heavenly Father and made for Him to love. Nothing you do can add one ounce of love to the infinite love God already has for you. Nothing you do can subtract one ounce of love from His overflowing heart.

THE WORK OF GOD'S LOVE IN US

When we accept this wonderful truth that God loves us infinitely and unconditionally, three tremendous things happen inside us.

First, we begin to value ourselves as God values us. We treat ourselves better. We take better care of ourselves. We seek to become all that we were created to be. We recognize our potential, and we seek to develop it.

When you fully embrace and grow in your awareness of God's love for you, you are set free to explore all that you might become and do.

Second, we grow in confidence. We have an increasing ability to trust our loving heavenly Father to provide for us, care for us, and preserve us. We have less fear of failure, less fear of rejection, less fear of loss. The Bible says we become increasingly "perfected" by God's love. His love casts out fear and torment (see 1 John 4:17–18). We are freed up emotionally to become all that we have been created to be. We no longer fear what others may say about us, say to us, or do to us. We no longer cave in to peer pressure. We no longer strive to live up to the expectations of other people.

When you fully embrace and grow in your awareness of God's love for you, you are set free to fully express your own wonderful self!

Third, we have a much greater ability to give love to others, and a greater capacity to receive love from others. When you fully embrace and grow in your awareness of God's love for you, you are set free to fully express your love to others in ways that are godly and pure.

KNOW WHAT YOU NEED FROM OTHER PEOPLE

Everyone needs to be loved by someone. We certainly want to feel the love of God, but we also want to be loved by people! As a little boy once said, "I need to feel love from somebody with skin on."

Danger bells should go off in us, however, if we find ourselves thinking that another person's love will *complete* us.

Nobody completes you—only God.

Other people might complement you—as in, help you build on your strengths or compensate for your weaknesses. Other people might compliment you—encouraging you by noticing your good qualities. But no human being is capable of single-handedly completing you, no matter how much that person may want to or try to. God has designed us so that it takes multiple people around us to meet our emotional needs, and so that only He is capable of meeting our spiritual needs.

God wants us to need a "body" of people (see 1 Corinthians 12:12–26), each of whom brings her gifts and abilities to bear on the relationship she has with us. God wants us to give to a body of people, too, bestowing on them our unique gifts and abilities. We are to have varying levels of intimacy with a variety of people, in a variety of areas.

I often encourage people, "Staff your weakness." This advice is good not only for business and ministry, but also for a person's personal life. Surround yourself with people who know what you don't know, who can do what you can't do, who can create what you can't create.

I am not a singer, but I definitely have that on the list of things I'm going to be able to do well once I'm in heaven. I know the tremendous role that music can have in ushering people into the presence of God. I would love to be able to sing and lead worship. But knowing that singing isn't my gift, I am eager to find those who *do* have a gift in leading praise and worship, and who have a heart that beats with mine when it comes to ministry purpose and passion.

A friend of mine recently celebrated, within a matter of weeks, her fiftieth birthday and her twenty-fifth wedding anniversary. She came to me griping, "I can't believe my husband didn't do anything special!" I laughed. At first, she thought I was laughing at the fact that he hadn't done anything special, and frankly, she didn't think it was very funny. I said, "No! I'm laughing at *you* because after all these years, you are still thinking that he might do something special to honor your birthday or anniversary. He hasn't done anything in the last twenty-four years. Why did you think he would now?"

My friend might have been hurt by my honest evaluation if I hadn't gone on to say, "What do you wish he would have done?" She named a couple of things. I said, "Great! Do those things! Plan that cruise and buy that dress, and on the last night of the cruise, when you are wearing that dress, sincerely and sweetly pull out the bracelet with the diamond pavé heart you wish he would have purchased for you and say, 'Sweetie, I know this is what you wanted to give to me, but you just didn't have time to shop for it.' He'll feel relieved. You'll feel pleased. And you both will have a wonderful time celebrating these milestones of life."

Now her husband had the financial means to pay for a cruise, a beautiful dress, and a bracelet with a diamond heart—and I know him well enough to know that he would be pleased for her to do this. You know your own situation. Evaluate it. Seek a way to meet your needs by involving, rather than repelling, those you love and value.

COMMUNICATE WHAT YOU NEED

A basic approach to communicating what you need is this:

- *Identify what you need from a specific person.* Part of having a vision for what you need or what needs to be done is knowing what is in keeping with the Word of God. God will not honor your pursuit of something that is contrary to His commands. The good news is that no genuinely good things are outside the realm of what God authorizes. All that has lasting benefit and eternal purpose is within the realm of possibility. Make sure that what you want is for the highest and best—not only in your life, but in the lives of those with whom you live, worship, and work. Get a clear vision of what is necessary and desirable.

- *Put it down in writing.* This is primarily for your own benefit. Sometimes we fail to see all that is necessary and desirable until we put it down in black and white and study what we have written. You may need to add or subtract from your initial vision. Having the statement in writing gives you a reference. It also sets a standard so that you truly know when you have acquired what you have desired.

- *Put your specific needs into the context of your greater vision for your life.* Know why you need this person to help in a certain way. Know what role she plays in the big picture—helping you reach goals related to who you want to become and what you want to accomplish.

- *Heed the vision in your own life.* Don't expect others to do what you aren't doing. Don't expect others to display a character higher than your character. Don't expect others to be generous when you are stingy, to be gracious when you are unkind, to be affectionate when you are cold, to show respect when you are demeaning, to applaud when you are critical. Model the behavior that you desire to see in others. Live out your highest character goals.

- *Encourage others to run with you toward the vision.* Share your vision and determine who will run with you toward achieving that vision. Not everybody will want precisely what you want. But somebody will!

THREE NEEDS YOU MAY BE OVERLOOKING

There are three additional needs that every person has, but which are often overlooked:

1. Sufficient downtime. I'm not talking about vegetating in front of a television set. The average American now spends twenty hours a week in front of a TV screen, and even more hours in front of a computer screen. That's not downtime. Downtime is time when you can think or meditate or reflect in solitude. Some people enjoy soft background music or praise songs. Downtime may involve a walk alone in a garden or park, time in the middle of the night in the overstuffed chair in the den, or a quiet half-hour in the middle of the afternoon, lying on a sofa and staring at the ceiling. Give yourself time to sort things out mentally, to create, to muse, to dream, to weigh possibilities and come up with options.

2. A safe place. Find a corner of the world in which you feel secure and emotionally safe. The Bible tells about a powerful man named Samson who got into huge trouble because he laid his head in an unsafe place, the lap of a woman named Delilah (see Judges 16)! You need to have a place you can go to encounter God. It might be a quiet corner in the church down the street from your workplace. It might be a small table in the library stacks at the back of the sixth floor. It might be a bench in the garden by the pond. The safe place is a place where you can openly, and verbally, ask questions of God. Asking the questions aloud gives you added insight into yourself—sometimes we don't know what we really believe, feel, or desire, until we hear our own ideas spoken from our own mouth. The safe place is a place where you can relax and open your mind and heart to God's response to you.

3. A means of flushing the negatives. Every person needs a means or method of flushing their own negative emotions from their soul. How do you express your anger? How do you vent your frustrations? How do you quell the rising tide of bitterness you feel in your soul? How do you get rid of feelings of hatred or vengeance?

Don't be afraid to voice your negative feelings to God. He can handle any choice of words and any degree of negativity you throw at Him! Read through the book of Psalms in the Bible and you'll see a man of passionate emotions telling God exactly how he feels and exactly how he wants God to deal with his enemies. The psalms of David also reflect tremendous peace of soul as David again and again comes to the realization that God is trust-worthy and that God is working at all times for his ultimate good.

When we get rid of all that stains and taints us and reach the point where we are willing to trust God in all things to do what is for our ulti-mate best . . . we find peace.

JOURNALING

I am a firm believer in writing down what I am feeling, not only as a way of recording my emotions, but also as a way of working out ideas, recording questions, identifying problems, and exploring various issues I desire to bring to resolution. As I read through my old journal, I found certain emotions being expressed repeatedly. I questioned virtually every-thing in my life. I voiced my pain and sorrow. I struggled to make sense of things that made no sense. I battled a desire to flee far away and yet at the same time, battled a desire to force decisions and resolution. My journal reflected great inner conflict at some points. But as I read on, I also came to pages that revealed other emotions. Things were starting to make sense. I felt more positive. I was filled with love for God and had abounding joy at His presence. I was at peace with those who had hurt me or frustrated me. I was finding answers and solutions.

We need to vent how we feel, or those feelings will build up in us to the point of explosion or decay. We will find ourselves either railing at other people or wallowing in our own bitterness and self-pity. Neither is healthy! Writing your feelings gives them a sense of validity, and that's important. After all, they are *your* feelings.

Find a way of venting what you feel, as you feel it, in a way that works for you and brings you to the point of trusting God wherever you are.

THE URGENCY OF THE NEED

We often say we *need* things that really are simply things we desire. We need to drink water, eat food, sleep, and so forth. If we are in relationship with others, and especially if we have young children, there are some things we need to do for our welfare and the welfare of those around us. There are also things we *want* to do for others. In return, there are some things we need to receive from others, and some things we may want to receive. When it comes to needs and wants, it's important to know the difference. What is vital? What is necessary? Those are needs. What is desirable? What is beneficial? Those are wants.

Give some thought to the issues in your life right now. Make a list of things you know you need, things you believe you have to have or do eventually, and things you want to do someday.

Reflect upon what you have written. Are your needs really needs, or are they desires?

Often, we feel a desperate longing for things we don't truly need. When you are desperate for a "want-to" in your life, take caution. Your desperation may drive you to do foolish things.

ONE ISSUE AT A TIME

Are you feeling a little overwhelmed at this point?

Are you wondering if you will ever know yourself well enough to make good choices and right decisions?

Let me encourage you not to take on too many issues in your life at one time. Take on one issue now. Explore one set of emotions down the line.

How does a person eat an elephant?

One bite at a time.

That's how we should approach analyzing our needs, our circumstances, and all other areas of our identity.

You didn't become who you are in a day.

You won't fully understand yourself in a day.

The discovery process never ends, and it should never be hurried. Ask God to reveal to you all you need to know, when you need to know it, and especially what you need to know for the next step He wants you to take.

Move beyond
Loss

9

LOSE WITHOUT LOSING
YOUR IDENTITY

*Y*ou aren't what you own.

Or are you?

To at least some degree, we each define ourselves—rightly or wrongly—by what we have and don't have.

Married: we *have* a spouse.

Parent: we *have* a child.

Home: we *have* an address we call our own, whether it is a mansion or a one-room apartment.

Work: we *have* a job or a business or a career.

Hobby: we *have* something we do for fun.

Service: we *have* a church that we attend, or we have a charity to which we contribute our money, time, or talent.

We *have* dreams, goals, and desires. We *have* friends. We *have* a list of accomplishments or failures that tend to shadow us.

We *have* a life—and to a great extent, the life we "possess" is what defines us.

But what happens if you lose a part of what you have?

What happens to your identity, your self-definition?

Who are you in the face of a loss, and how do you overcome an external loss without losing your own internal identity?

LOSS IS A PART OF LIFE

The truth is, every person experiences loss at some time and to some degree. Some losses are simply woven into life and are considered normal—children go to school and eventually grow up and leave home, friends move away, companies go out of business, parents retire, beloved grandparents die. Even though they're a normal part of life, no loss is ever truly *desirable*. If it were desirable, it would be called a gain instead of a loss!

Because some degree of loss is inevitable, the challenge that every person faces when it comes to loss is threefold:

- Minimizing the pain
- Learning something good in the process
- Hanging onto a strong sense of self

There are two overriding principles about loss that we need to recognize:

1. Loss takes us to our core. First, let's openly admit that loss hurts. There are some losses that seem insurmountable or are so painful they seem unbearable. These losses take us to the very core of our deepest fears. The loss might be separation or divorce from someone we love deeply, the death or kidnapping of a child, a paralyzing accident, or the bankruptcy of a business or farm that has been in the family for generations. Each of these losses can encompass a person's entire life and identity. Each can be deeply wounding, and could produce painful memories for decades to come. We should never dismiss the pain of loss.

People tend to express pain in different ways—some wail and scream and shout; others withdraw and become reclusive for a while. Some people are eager to tell others about their pain; others fall silent. Some people are ashamed of loss, or ashamed of feeling pain. Others don't care who knows about a loss and are eager to receive help, prayers, and encouragement from anybody and everybody.

Take a little time to determine how you tend to respond to loss. Reflect on how you treat others who are experiencing loss and whether your treatment of them is fair, empathetic, and beneficial.

2. Loss varies in intensity and scope over time. Loss is always filtered through the lens of personal perspective. We give our losses a "value" or a "weight." We may see a loss as a knockout punch or a glancing blow. As hours, days, and weeks pass, our evaluation may change, and likely will change.

"Big" losses tend to generate the most emotional pain, but we must never discount the accumulative impact that a series of "small" losses can have. Several small losses can add up to a tremendously large loss.

I know this to be true in my own life. I once went through a period of several months in which my family and I experienced hit after hit after hit. One hit would have been sufficient. Repeated hits created a serious challenge to everything we knew as stability, security, and identity.

In the heat of those months of loss, the weight of the losses was enormous. The losses were great, but the emotional weight we attached to them changed over time. Some of the hits we took became more consequential and important over time; other hits were forgotten as life moved on. Some of the pain associated with the losses took months, even years to heal. The pain associated with other losses healed quickly as circumstances changed.

What's important to recognize is that all loss is temporary! Even the most catastrophic loss is only for a season. Circumstances and situations and people change.

Hearts heal.

Perspectives change.

New relationships develop.

Fortunes can be restored; possessions can be acquired.

Love and hope and faith can be reborn.

[All loss is temporary!]

LOSS IS GOVERNED BY PERCEPTION

Your perception about a loss directly impacts the pain you experience. What you consider to be a tremendously damaging loss may be taken in stride by another person, and vice versa.

I recently heard about a woman who was married to a prominent man in their community. The husband died of a heart attack after an intense business meeting in which very large sums of money were at stake and opinions were sharply divided. This woman found herself a widow at the age of fifty. One of her friends came to her with an armload of flowers and attempted to console her by telling her what a fine man her husband had been. She didn't get far. The new widow stopped her and said, "I appreciate your good intentions, and I truly appreciate your friendship all these years, but you really don't understand how I am feeling. I have never really confided in you about my pain or my relationship with my husband. The truth is, this last week has been the first week in twenty-seven years that I have not been routinely belittled or criticized at least a dozen times a day for a wide variety of faults, from the way I dress to the way I cook. This last week was the first time in a very long time that I got up every morning with peace in my heart and went to bed each night with joy in my soul. My husband was an accomplished man, a good provider, and a good business leader. He was as good a father as he knew to be. But he was not a loving husband, and I really won't miss him as much as you may think I will."

Now, I hope that this widow didn't mean everything she said in that moment and that she was simply attempting to diminish her loss, which can be a normal response to grief. Many times a person who experiences loss will attempt to discount the thing that has been lost, or to criticize the person who has walked away, in an attempt to diminish the pain or the consequences.

I also recognize, however, that not everything we perceive to be a tragedy or a loss in another person's life is actually a loss from *her* perspective. This widow's response is an extreme case, but the principle is one that covers a wide variety of situations. One person might see the downsizing from a mansion to a condominium as a loss, but the person who is doing the downsizing may see it as an extremely liberating experience. One person might see the loss of a job as a tremendous blow, but the person who has lost the job may see it as the opportunity to become an entrepreneur and start his own business.

Certainly not everything turns out to be as devastating in the long run as it may appear to be in the short run. What may seem to be a tragedy in the heat of the moment may turn out to be a tremendous blessing five years down the line. It is how we perceive a loss and how we continue to perceive a loss that truly shapes how we will deal with that loss.

"But," you may be saying, "some things cannot be replaced. The loss is real. It doesn't matter how you think about the loss—the home, or person, or dream is gone."

True, but perception makes a huge difference in how you will recover and how long the recovery will take.

> Perception makes a huge difference in how you will recover and how long the recovery will take.

You may have lost your home, but do you perceive that life will never be the same, or that a new and better home may be in your future?

You may have lost your marriage, but do you perceive that your family is damaged forever, or that a deeply satisfying and fulfilling life can still be yours?

You may have lost a fortune, but do you perceive that you will never recover from the loss, or that you can still live and produce and create a new life, and perhaps even gain a greater fortune?

Your perception will determine how you move forward. Never lose sight of the fact that your response to loss is the most important factor when it comes to rebuilding your life.

Identify your loss. Define it as fully as you can, with all the ramifications you believe it holds for your life and the lives of those close to you. Then turn your loss into a prayer. Ask God to reverse the loss in His way, in His timing, and for your eternal benefit. Then stand back, and watch Him begin to work!

10

MAKE THE DECISION TO GET UP AND GO FORWARD

$\mathcal{M}$any labels were placed on my life from the tragic experiences of my childhood and beyond. People determined that I would never be whole, happy, and satisfied. I had two choices: I could accept that determination and live less than the life God designed for me, or I could make a decision to rely upon Him to do what His Word says He will do. I chose the latter. That one decision to rely upon God changed my life. I found out that you are not necessarily a product of where you came from or what has happened to you.

> You can choose to get up, pick up whatever it is that is holding you captive, and move forward toward the fullness of all God has for you.

What I am saying is that you can choose to live according to God's design for you rather than according to the way mankind defines you. You can choose to get up, pick up whatever is holding you captive, and move forward toward the fullness of all God has for you, not limited by the labels man has placed on you.

RESIST THE RESISTANCE

Resistance is a fact of life. The apostle Paul wrote to the Christians in the Greek city of Philippi, "I press on toward the goal to win the prize" (Philippians 3:14 NIV). There's a *pressing* required for the things of lasting value on this earth and into eternity. Those things that come quickly often fade just as quickly.

Are you aware that most of those who win big lottery prizes are broke within five years? Why? Because they don't have a foundation of good money-management skills. And how is it that a person gains good money-management skills? By pressing forward day by day, learning to manage small amounts of money and then increasingly larger amounts of money.

It is in the struggles of life that we become strong. It is in dealing with our lack and trusting God for His provision that we grow in faith and in our ability to handle provision.

The Bible tells us that the enemy of Eve's soul came calling on her in the Garden of Eden with a simple lie: she could eat one piece of fruit from one particular tree and suddenly be as wise as God (see Genesis 3:1–7). The enemy of your soul is likely to come at you with the same deceit: do this one simple thing and everything will be fixed.

Life doesn't operate according to simple fixes. It functions on the basis of long-term obedience, faith, and acts of love and service. It functions on a moment of life-changing faith, followed up by a life of faith-changing moments!

REFUSE TO LIE DOWN IN EXCUSES OR LIES

The Word of God tells a story about Jesus going to a pool of water in Jerusalem that had been given the name "Bethesda"—referring to God's mercy and grace. The pool was associated with healing miracles. The springs that fed that particular pool occasionally bubbled dramatically, and the people believed that an angel was stirring the water and that the first person into the pool after this happened would be healed of whatever ailed him or her. Scores of people were carried to the edges of the pool every day in hopes that the waters might bubble up with healing power (see John 5:1–9).

Jesus encountered a man there who had been lying by the pool, having had an infirmity for thirty-eight years. I don't know how long you've been living the way you are living, hoping for a dramatic change or a touch of God's power in your life, but I do know some people who have lived that way for thirty-eight years. They are miserable and paralyzed in their misery.

Jesus saw this man in his condition, just as God sees you in your condition today. Don't miss this point: Jesus found this man by the pool— the man didn't seek and find Jesus. God isn't looking for someone who occupies a certain position in life or who is in a certain location. He's looking for a person who is hungry for His presence.

The truth is that God is searching for you, and with far more urgency than you have ever searched for Him. God isn't lost and doesn't need to be found. We are the ones who are lost and need finding.

> The truth is that God is searching for you, and with far more urgency than you have ever searched for Him.

Jesus asked the man at the pool of Bethesda a simple question: "Do you want to be made well?"

That may seem like a silly question, but many people who are down, discouraged, or sick do not want to be well—not really. They have grown accustomed to the pity and care they receive as sick people. They have come to enjoy being waited upon, catered to, and accommodated in special ways. They enjoy being the center of attention and, subconsciously at least, they believe that if they truly become well, whole, self-reliant, responsible adults, they will lose more than they gain. The question, "Do you want to be made well?" is one of the most potent questions you can ever ask another person or yourself.

The man did not answer Jesus directly, but rather, made this excuse: "I don't have anyone who will put me into the pool when the water is stirred up. Somebody always gets there before me" (see John 5:1–9).

This man was lying on a bed of excuses and faulty thinking. He was not unlike many people I have encountered. There are at least five major "beds" on which people lie sick and paralyzed. All of them involve faulty thinking, error, or excuses.

The bed of a limited label. There's no way to sum up all of who you are in a single word, but many people try to do just that, giving themselves labels and then refusing to peel off those labels or add others. They firmly believe they are stupid . . . boring . . . ugly . . . incapable . . . unworthy . . . unlovable . . . sinful . . . useless . . . a worm. Far more people define themselves with negative labels than with positive ones. Are you lying on a label that you believe defines you and your potential? Jesus said to the man by the pool of Bethesda, "Rise, take up thy bed, and walk" (John 5:8). I believe He would say those same words to you today. Get up! Roll up that excuse and move on in your life!

The bed of poor assumptions. Are you lying down on a bed of assumption that you can never be, won't be, shouldn't be, are incapable of being, or aren't worthy of being something? Are you assuming that you will never get well, never recover, never be able to pay all your bills, never be educated, never be skilled, never be in charge of your own life? Get up! Roll up that bed of faulty thinking and find a qualified and godly advisor who can help you sort out your finances and live by a budget, get the skills you need, or make the important or pressing decisions you are facing,

The bed of pessimism. Do you tend to see more negatives than positives in life? Do you see faults more than strengths? Are you looking for the next bad thing that might happen, rather than expecting tomorrow to be brighter? Pessimism breeds discouragement, depression, and despair. You have a choice to make about how you see things and how you will respond to life. Choose to believe. Choose to be hopeful about your future. Get up! Roll up that bed of discouragement and get on with your life!

I learned many years ago that we can choose to resist everything that tries to hold us back. Abuse and abandonment are two conditions that often produce a victim mentality in a person, especially if the person experienced abuse or abandonment as a young child. Resist giving in to a victim mind-set! Addiction and temptation can come against you in unexpected ways and at inopportune times. Resist giving in to old patterns of behavior.

Feelings of rejection and low self-esteem can pull you down just when you are starting to feel "up." Resist! Resist, resist, resist. Say no to everything that attempts to discourage you or diminish your potential. This takes an act of your will. If you feel weak, ask God to impart to you the ability to resist.

The bed of impossible standards. Do you think in terms of all or nothing? Do you think some things will *always* be the way they are, that some things can *never* change, or that there are certain standards that *must* be met for you to be accepted and loved? If you hold to all-or-nothing ideas, you set yourself up for failure. Choose to be realistic about life, and then choose to get up and get moving. Do what you can do and don't get bogged down by what you can't accomplish. Don't allow yourself to become paralyzed by the specter of possible failure.

The bed of comparison. Do you compare yourself to others and come away feeling bad about yourself? Do you tear others down in order to make yourself look better? God doesn't compare His children. He loves each of us for the unique person He created us to be. He doesn't grade on a curve. He has plenty of rewards for each person, without ever short-changing anyone.

If you lie down on a bed of comparison, you will always be discouraged to some degree, because you'll always be able to find someone who is smarter, richer, more beautiful, stronger, faster, or more capable than you are. Very few people are number one in anything in the world, and those who are rarely stay in that position for long. Don't let that fact discourage you. Know that God doesn't ask you to be number one in any category of life. He asks only that you love Him, love others, do what you know is right, and be the most authentic *you* that you can possibly be. Get up! Roll up your detrimental comparative thinking and move forward in your life!

Speak to yourself by name and tell yourself to get up in every area where you are lying down . . . *now!*

I have been to many boxing matches. I will never forget one in particular where the champion, who came across as very arrogant, was suddenly and unexpectedly knocked down. The referee stood over him with the count—"One . . . two . . . three!" Around "seven" or "eight," the champion began to get back up and gather his composure. He came back with a vengeance and defeated his opponent badly. He "put a hurt on him!"

Choose to be like that boxer—not in his arrogance, but in his will to get up. Take up your bed of impossible standards and move forward in your life!

11

REGAIN YOUR SIGNIFICANCE

A friend recently told me about a midnight call she received from a distraught woman whose husband had died an hour earlier on the operating table at a nearby hospital. My friend said, "I didn't know where to begin, Paula. She was crying hysterically, shouting angrily at God, telling me she loved me, and talking about selling her Winnebago, all in forty-five seconds. All I could do was say her name over and over in a calm, soothing voice. Along with her name, I said, 'Breathe.'"

When we experience loss, we hurt. Our first response is nearly always emotional, and the emotions are often varied and intense. At times, we can be so overwhelmed by the loss that we feel as if we are drowning in a sea of sorrow. If such intense emotions continue, we can become paralyzed emotionally.

Many of us feel diminished by loss. What we once had or did is suddenly obsolete—the job is gone, the family is gone, the entire neighborhood may be gone. . . . The role we once played is no longer necessary or available—and with the loss comes a lack of purpose, responsibility, and value.

Men especially struggle with their identity when they lose their jobs, their virility, or their health. Women especially struggle with their identity when they lose a spouse or children. Why? Because men often find their identity and significance in what they *do*—their work, accomplishments, acquisitions, paychecks, sexual prowess, and ability to conquer enemies and complete tasks. Men feel significant when they provide what others need physically, materially, and financially. Women, in contrast, find their identity and significance in their *relationships*—their husbands, children, other family members, friends, and others who turn to them for nurture. Women feel significant when they provide what others need emotionally.

Significance is vitally linked to identity. When a person doesn't feel significant, he begins to feel unlovable and without value. But in reality, he is still vitally important and just as worthy of love as ever—it's only his *self-perception* that has changed.

According to God's Word, every person is significant to God solely because that person is alive on the earth! Every person has value and is worthy of love. The New Testament makes it very clear that God so loved the world that He made it possible for "whosoever will" to accept His plan of forgiveness, abundant life, and His eternal love (see John 3:16). Nobody is excluded from the category of "whosoever." Everybody has an equal opportunity to "will"—to say yes to the offer of forgiveness and eternal love that God offers.

> Every person has value and is worthy of love.

One of the most important questions you can ask yourself is this: "If I never _____ again, will God still love me?"

I asked myself this question at a time when I was feeling overwhelmed, frustrated, and discouraged about some things in my life. "Paula," I said aloud, "if you never preach another sermon, will God still love you?"

I wrestled with that question for quite a while before answering myself. Did my value lie in my preaching ability? Did my worth to God lie in the effectiveness of my preaching or the service of my ministry? Did God love me more after I preached a good sermon, or conversely, did God love me less after I preached a less-than-my-best sermon? Would God love me less if I gave up preaching altogether? You may think the answers to such questions would be obvious to me or would come quickly. Not so. I considered these questions at length until I was finally able to say with deep conviction, "Of course, God will love you, Paula, if you never preach another sermon!"

You may phrase a question about your significance a little differently than I did:

- "If I never _____, will God love me?"
- "If I fail at _____, will God love me?"
- "If I can't _____, will God love me?"
- "If I lose _____, will God love me?"

Although there may be times when you don't *feel* lovable, let me assure you that God counts you as lovable, regardless of what you accomplish or don't accomplish, perform or don't perform, achieve or don't achieve (see 1 John 4:10). His love is not linked to any works on your part, either good or bad.

In times of loss, you must make a deliberate effort to guard against feelings of insignificance and discouragement. It is very important to continue to get up each morning and find somebody who needs something you can provide. Your job may be gone, but you can volunteer to help others until you find a new job. Your children may have left home and live in another state, but you can go to any number of agencies that specialize in helping children and volunteer your nurturing skills and love. Your spouse may have left you, but I guarantee you this, there's somebody at the nearest nursing home or hospital who needs your care and attention.

Find something to do.

Find someone to whom you can give what you do have.

And trust God to love you at all times and in all situations.

THE PROCESS OF LOSS AND RECOVERY

Loss and recovery are a process. The immediate need when dealing with loss is survival. People who are in survival mode are desperate for miracles. They need answers and long for immediate recovery.

The Bible offers us a tremendous example of people who were in survival mode. If you read through the book of Exodus, you will find that the Israelites went from one crisis to the next. They experienced one plague and hardship after the next as slaves in Egypt. Then when they fled from slavery in Egypt, they faced a pursuing army sent by Pharaoh, and the barrier of the Red Sea. Even after miraculously crossing the Red Sea, they faced lack of water, lack of food, a never-ending wilderness, and the prospect of taking on giants in the land that God had promised as their new home. They needed an entire string of miracle "fixes." Their story illustrates the three stages involved as a person experiences and recovers from loss:

1. *Not enough.* In Egypt, the Israelites never had full satisfaction. As slaves, they didn't have nearly enough physical provision, and they didn't have the opportunity to worship freely. They were slaves with a slave mind-set. Many people today are lacking in emotional provision. They suffer from extreme loneliness, feelings of rejection or alienation, disappointment or depression. They feel no joy in their hearts. They describe themselves as feeling "needy"—as if they can't get enough love, enough understanding or compassion from others, enough friendship, and—nearly always at the core—enough of God's presence.

2. *Just enough.* In the wilderness, the Israelites had just enough. They were given sufficient food for each day. They were given sufficient guidance for the next step in their journey. They were given victories over their enemies, one group at a time. The Israelites never conquered or laid claim to the wilderness. Their experience there was trudging through, one year at a time. Many people exist in a "just enough" state today, both materially and emotionally. They feel as if they are trudging through their days, trapped in a routine that seems endless. They never really feel on top of life, but rather, as if they are just barely hanging on.

3. *More than enough.* In the Promised Land, the Israelites eventually experienced more than enough. They entered a land "flowing with milk and honey" (Numbers 13:27), in which their crops could prosper, permanent homes could be built, and they could experience full freedom to worship. A life that is marked by "more than enough" is the life to which

most people aspire. We all want to feel love, satisfaction, fulfillment, and purpose in overflowing quantities.

Where are you in this spectrum? Are you in serious lack? Do you scrape by from day to day, week to week, month to month? Do you have more than enough so that you can enjoy sharing your abundance with others?

Trouble occurs when people get stuck in the "not enough" phase. They get hooked on their need for miracles. They go from place to place, church to church, and person to person, looking for today's "fix" that will meet their immediate emotional need. Those who are in the "not enough" stage face the challenge of being willing to leave a loss behind and move toward a new future. The person in a town where the unemployment rate is astronomical, with no job opportunities, has to be willing to acquire new skills and perhaps even relocate, which can be frightening if all he or she has ever known is that environment and experience. The person in an abusive relationship has to be willing to walk away and find shelter for herself and her children, which is frightening if it means giving up the only home she has and the only provider she knows. Fear can keep a person trapped forever in a "not enough" life!

Is there a danger for those who are wandering in the "just enough" stage of their recovery? Yes. Those in this stage face a daily life that can become routine and monotonous. Like the Israelites, they have enough manna, but they need to get up every morning and gather it before the dew dries out, and they have to fix it and eat it before the next morning. Life takes on a sameness. There's no one cracking a whip, but there's also a new discipline that has to be walked out.

A person in this phase might be tempted to fantasize about the past, which seems far better in retrospect than it ever was in reality. The Israelites craved the cucumbers, melons, and onions of Egypt as they ate their diet of manna. They said, "What are we doing out here in the wilderness? Slavery surely must have been a better deal" (see Numbers 11:20). They focused on where they had been rather than where they were going. If you aren't careful at this stage, you may very well start thinking that "not enough" is better than the hope of "more than enough."

Countless victims of abuse fall into this trap. They return to their abusers because life free of the abuse is unknown and uncomfortable, and they have little ability to foresee a brighter future in a healthy relationship.

As the Israelites were about to enter the Promised Land and leave the time of "just enough" in the wilderness, God spoke to them through Moses. He said they were literally to write down key principles of God and "bind" them to their bodies, to bind certain principles to their lives and teach these principles to their children (see Deuteronomy 6:6–9). These principles covered what they could do, what they couldn't do, what they could have, and what they couldn't have.

The principles came with consequences. Observing the commands of God was linked to tremendous blessings. Disobedience was linked to terrible devastation (see Deuteronomy 28).

Abiding by the principles of God resulted in the Israelites' experiencing "more than enough" in their Promised Land. The same is true for us today.

If you continue to build your life according to God's principles and patterns, you will eventually get to a place of blessing—a place of "more than enough." I have no doubt about that!

If you build a structure with consistency and perseverance, even if you build only a little a day, you eventually will have a completed building. If you continue to clean up the overwhelming mess after a major storm, you will eventually have clear ground to rebuild and replant. If you pay down on your debt long enough, you will come to a place of being debt-free and able to prosper financially, especially if you invest the money you were paying on debts into things that bring a good rate of return. If you eat well and exercise long enough and in the right ways, you will come to a place of being physically fit. If you continue to do the things that are necessary for a healthy self-concept, you will emerge with a stronger self identity and a better foundation for new relationships.

The danger at this point lies in thinking that you don't need to continue to live by godly, healthy principles once you arrive at your goal. If you want to enjoy your dream for many years to come, you need to maintain it. If you want to stay physically fit, you must continue to eat right and exercise. If you want to stay out of debt, you have to avoid continual spending splurges that drive you back into debt. If you want to stay emotionally healthy, you need to do the things that nurture, strengthen, and build up "self" to forge healthy relationships. I say it this way: "Don't stop dancing with the one who brought you to the prom." In other words, don't stop doing what you did to get to where you are now.

Don't become proud in your Promised Land, thinking that you have achieved or can maintain a status of "more than enough" in your own mental, physical, or spiritual strength. The Israelites knew they couldn't escape Egypt without God's miraculous intervention. They knew they couldn't make it through the wilderness without God's constant guidance, protection, and provision. They got into trouble once they were in the Promised Land only when they began to think that they could defend, build, and order their lives apart from God.

Know where you are in the process of loss and recovery. An honest inventory is your best safeguard against making the mistakes that can trip you up as you move from where you are to where you desire to be.

KNOW WHERE YOU ARE AND WHAT YOU FEEL

There's tremendous value in knowing where you are in the process of loss and recovery, and to identifying how you are feeling. I call it "locating." When you "locate," you know better how to pray, and also what to seek out or do.

Consider the possibilities described below. Find the stage you are at, then read the corresponding action point:

STAGE IN THE PROCESS	I FEEL INSIGNIFICANT (UNLOVABLE)	I FEEL SIGNIFICANT (LOVABLE)
Acute loss: not enough	Ask for help. You need help to get help beyond your loss; seek wise counsel about your future from a person of your own sex.	Make your move. You are ready to take a risk and go forward; seek wise counsel about your future from a person of your own sex.

STAGE IN THE PROCESS	I FEEL INSIGNIFICANT (UNLOVABLE)	I FEEL SIGNIFICANT (LOVABLE)
Maintaining after acute loss: "just enough"	Establish a series of rewards for yourself that are healthy and positive; find others to whom you can give yourself (time, talent, skills). Identify clear goals and put those goals on a timetable for accomplishing them.	Continue to reward yourself in positive ways. Continue to give to others of your time, talent, and skills. Identify clear goals and put your goals on a timetable for accomplishing them.
Beginning to make real progress toward "more than enough"	Expand your giving. Develop relationships that are interdependent, in which you can both give and receive.	Set new goals for giving. Bolster your interdependent relationships.

In each of these areas, women may want to identify specific *people* related to their goals and giving. Men may want to identify specific *tasks* they can do successfully in order to reach their goals.

ADDRESS YOUR FEELINGS

Address *all* of your feelings and make a strategy for dealing with them. I recommend that you:

- *Make a list of the emotions you are feeling.* There are no right or wrong emotions when you are hit with a loss. All emotions are valid. Next to each emotion put a rating of 1–10 indicating how intense the emotion is (1 is "low" and 10 is "high"). Keep a running list from week to week. Date your entries. You should be able to see a trend toward fewer and less intense negative emotions as the weeks pass.

If there are no changes, I strongly urge you to reach out for support and possibly even consult a Christian counselor.

- *Identify your needs.* Refer to your own needs analysis. Identify *all* the needs you face—physical, financial, material, emotional, and spiritual.
- *Identify ways to deal with your feelings and meet your needs.* Next to each emotion or need on your list, write down at least one option for meeting that need, *apart from the possibility of returning to your former state.* Ideally, identify more than one option.

When someone experiences a loss of identity, she can feel as if her soul is being torn apart. The pain is intense and yet sometimes difficult to isolate and define. Many people who are struggling with a loss of identity don't recognize what is going on inside them. They simply feel deeply frustrated, anxious, or uneasy.

These are dangerous emotions! They are the very emotions that often lead to substance abuse and addiction. The substances cover the feelings of anxiety. They mask them and enable you to feel better, at least temporarily. But using substances to deal with unsettling emotions is like putting a Band-Aid on a broken arm.

Only by confronting what you are feeling can you truly begin the process of transformation. Recognize that your emotions are often linked to a loss, and at the same time, recognize that all loss is temporary, and therefore, these emotions are temporary. Don't ignore your feelings. Rather, make a conscious, intentional decision to deal with your loss in a positive way that does *not* include destructive behaviors or the use of harmful substances. Find a safety valve to release the tension building in your heart.

For many people, the best safety valve is a form of physical activity. Consider taking up a new sport or adventure in your life. During a time of intense inner tension in my life, I took up tennis. I had never seriously played tennis before that time, and I thoroughly enjoyed slamming that tennis ball against a backboard and learning to serve with power. You may find walking or running to be a way of releasing tension. A friend of mine loves to swim, and she said about a stressful time in her life, "I'd swim when I got home from work—one lap for every negative encounter of the day. Sometimes I was in the pool for twenty minutes, slapping the negativity out of my life one stroke at a time, and sometimes I was in the pool for forty-five minutes!"

Don't let despair take hold. Make a decision that you can and will move forward with your life in a positive way. Take steps toward something that restores and builds your confidence. And don't forget to breathe, literally and figuratively. Give yourself permission to be human. Take a deep, relaxing gulp of oxygen and count to three as you slowly let it out. Breathe again, and live again!

12

EIGHT VITAL STEPS TO RECOVERY

I feel as if something in me died," she said.

In truth, something had "died"—her marriage. Her husband had walked out on her to be with a woman twenty years younger.

"It would have been easier if there had been a real death," she added.

I had no doubt she was right. Divorce is often the "living death" of a relationship; it has all the pain of lasting separation without the closure of burial.

All loss of relationship is a death of sorts and involves a grieving process. You may be in denial at the outset. You will no doubt feel confusion, anger, and sadness at varying points. The good news is that if you allow yourself to fully experience each stage of the recovery process, you can arrive at a point where you feel strong enough to dream again and to design a new future for yourself.

> With God, you have all you need to walk into your future.

When you lose something important to you, remember that you have not lost God, and He certainly hasn't lost you. Your relationship with God through Christ Jesus is fixed. It cannot be altered (see 2 Corinthians 1:21–22.) What you have, therefore, is far more potent than what you have lost. With God, you have all you need to walk into your future.

There are eight steps that most people need to go through sequentially to fully recover from a significant loss.

STEP #1: WITHDRAW FOR A PURPOSE

This first step may be necessary to ensure some degree of safety and shelter for yourself. Your home may have been washed away in the flood waters—you must find shelter. You may be in a situation that requires you to flee from your home and find a place that is safer and more secure. The need for safety and shelter is very strong in times of loss.

You may feel a strong need to withdraw from the world at large when faced with a loss, and that's okay. Just make sure it's for a limited time. Don't beat yourself up for escaping momentarily from the intensity of the loss. Even strong, ferocious animals, when wounded, retreat to their caves to nurse their wounds.

Withdraw for a purpose—to spend time with God and to gain a new perspective on your life. Read your Bible and talk to God about your pain, but also about other things in your life, from the ridiculously trivial to the eternally sublime. Don't run from your life. . . . Run to God. He'll help you in ways you can't even imagine when you are adrift on a sea of pain.

> Don't run from your life. . . . Run to God.

STEP #2: TAKE TIME TO GRIEVE YOUR LOSS

Give yourself permission to mourn your loss and to cry when you feel like crying. Express your sorrow to God. Ask Him to heal your broken heart. This is prayer: communicating with God on a very personal, intimate level.

Grieving nearly always includes some form of anger. Find constructive ways to express or vent your anger. Take a chainsaw to a fallen tree. Run a mile every morning. Enroll in a kick-boxing class and pretend the punching bag is the devil.

Be very intentional about finding positive ways of expressing your anger. Yelling, even into a pillow, solves nothing, and if your yelling is vented at people around you, it can be destructive. Doing damage to property may seem temporarily therapeutic, but in the long run, it sets up a cycle that can be anything but beneficial. Don't kick the dog. If you truly believe you have been denied justice, seek justice in ways that are legal and moral. Express to God how angry you are, and ask Him to exact justice on your behalf and to restore to you all that He desires for you to have.

Grieving also involves dealing with some very practical matters, often the sorting of possessions. One of the best things you can do as part of your grieving process is to sort out what is wisely kept and what should be tossed in the trash. A woman whose fiancé left her at the altar said a lot in just one sentence: "I kept the beautiful, inscribed music box and threw out the old love letters and photos." She kept what she believed could have a positive place in her future, and threw away what did not.

Another woman who had been through a divorce said, "After my former husband had taken everything from the house that was legally his, I went through the house from top to bottom. I kept some things for my children's sake, such as photographs, but I discarded everything I had wished for years that my husband would have trashed and hadn't—boxes of things that he had cared about too much to toss but didn't care enough about to take with him. And then, I trashed all of my old lingerie and nightwear and bought myself new things!"

People have different timetables for dealing with material possessions after a loss. Sort things out when you feel ready, not when others around you pressure you to deal with your material goods.

Grieving involves feelings of disappointment, frustration, and anxiety. Perhaps the best remedy for dealing with these feelings is to write in a journal how you are feeling, and eventually, what you begin to dream for your future. Express yourself in as much detail as possible. Once these things are written, you won't feel the same need to rehearse your feelings repeatedly in your mind. In addition, you'll also be able to gain some perspective by seeing your fears, anger, and other emotions in writing. You'll likely find that, once your feelings are down on paper, you are better able to let go of your deepest fears, disappointments, and frustrations.

Look for trustworthy, stable people in whom you can confide and who have shoulders you can cry on. Seek out those who will help you materially or financially through your loss. Recognize, however, that their assistance is temporary. Appreciate what others offer you and do for you, but also set yourself on a path toward taking responsibility for your own life. You'll find that others are even *more* likely to help you if they perceive that you are on a path toward helping yourself and are eager to get beyond your loss and recover fully.

NOURISH YOURSELF

When you take a hit in your life, it is vital that you continue to nourish your physical body. The mind-body connection is stronger than most people realize. It seems that science reveals more and more about this with each passing month. The old saying is true—"You are what you eat!" The nutrients that you take into your body become fuel not only physically, but mentally as well. Make sure that you eat the right foods, in the right quantities, and in the right balance, especially when you are going through a crisis. Make sure that you are getting enough exercise and enough rest; both are critical to your maintaining overall health in times of great stress or crisis.

On a daily basis, strive to build strong health habits. Choose to eat right, sleep right, and exercise right—right now! It's been well documented that low blood sugar levels produce low energy and sluggish thinking, which in turn can feel like discouragement or even mild depression. Eating small protein-rich meals several times a day can do wonders for keeping blood-sugar levels even. The result is greater sustained energy throughout the day, sharper thinking, and a more positive outlook. Keep a protein bar or simple protein-rich foods—a hard-boiled egg, a cup of nonfat yogurt or cottage cheese, or a handful of nuts—available for snacking, rather than sugar-based sweets such as candy, cookies, soda drinks, pies, or cakes.

Just as you nourish your physical body, you need to nourish your emotions. For that I recommend a hearty laugh! The Bible tells us that a merry heart is good for a person, like good medicine (see Proverbs 17:22). Laughter produces chemicals in the brain—endorphins—that give a person a greater sense of well-being. Find out what makes you laugh, and treat yourself to a dose of that. Read something funny, listen to a comedy CD, or watch an old movie or television series. When I'm down, it's amazing how much better I feel after popping in a *Three Stooges* or *I Love Lucy* DVD and allowing myself to laugh at their crazy antics. If you have lost your ability to laugh at the silly things in life, do your best to regain that ability. Nobody should be so serious or so cynical that he loses his ability to belly-laugh.

Recall funny experiences in your past, and laugh at them.

Develop your own lightheartedness. Don't take yourself so seriously, or take on the weight of the world to the point that you lose sight of small pleasures and innocent joys.

Laugh at your own foibles and goofs. Several years ago, I was scheduled to pray prior to the dinner at a prestigious and very formal banquet. The person driving me to the event got lost on the way there and time was running out. I was too stressed to pay close attention to the state of my clothes as I walked to the platform and sat next to the most important person in the room. Little did I know that my dress was caught in my panty hose in the back, and it was "hiked up" significantly. Finally, somebody tapped me on the shoulder and told me what I needed to adjust in my appearance. Suffice it to say that that was a Christmas banquet those people will never forget. If I need a personal laugh, I simply recall that moment, or some other silly, crazy moment of my life!

In a situation like that, there's really no point in feeling embarrassed. What had happened was accidental, not intentional. It was funny and deserved a laugh. If you can't laugh at yourself, you'll find yourself less and less willing to take risks in life. At the same time, you'll make others feel much tenser because they'll pick up on your tension. Do your best. Expect the most. But be willing to laugh when you make honest mistakes or crazy goofs.

> Do your best. Expect the most. But be willing to laugh when you make honest mistakes or crazy goofs.

Create Your Own Retreat Space

Finding a place where you feel totally comfortable and fully free to orga-nize things to your liking is very important as you initially face recovery from a major loss.

Many people know these words from Psalm 23: "The Lord is my shepherd, I shall not want. He maketh me to lie down in green pastures: he leadeth me beside the still waters." Sometimes the Lord "maketh us" to retreat, to rest, to remove ourselves from the routine of our lives, so that we can fully recovery from the blows that have left us feeling wounded, disoriented, or exhausted.

Some time ago, I began to look for a "breathing place" or "watering hole"—a place decorated in my style, with my likes. I was facing some problems that threatened to overwhelm me. I needed a place where I could go sort things out, bit by bit, decision by decision, choice by choice. So I rented an apartment to use as a retreat, and having it has made a tremen-dous difference. When I'm there, I feel completely free to turn off my cell phone and structure my time the way I choose. It's really increased my abil-ity to hear from God what it is that He desires for me to do and not do.

The temptation in my life has always been to do, rather than not do. At times, it is very important for me to hear very clearly what God desires that I *not* take on or commit to. Had I tried to "stay in the fray" of my very busy work and home schedule, surrounded by people I dearly love pulling me in countless directions and feeling totally absorbed by each day's problems, I don't think I would have been able to see my way clearly. Areas where I was feeling weak and wounded would not have healed or been replenished as quickly.

What happens when we can't discern God's desires for us? What hap-pens when we don't give ourselves time to recuperate from issues or expe-riences that have sapped our emotional or physical strength? We make poor choices and weak decisions. We have very little forward motion in our lives. We tend to react out of our stress rather than respond out of our strength. None of those are good consequences!

"But," you may be saying, "I can't afford a place of retreat." Perhaps not, but the Lord can reveal to you a "space" where you can go and get away from pressure—even if it's for only an hour a day or a few hours on a weekend. It might be a public park bench by a pond, a stretch of public beach, or a balcony with a view. Ask God where your "still waters" and "green pastures" might be.

The bottom line is that you need to find a place where you have total freedom to "rest" emotionally. You need to be able to get away from the stressful circumstances and situations of life—periodically and perhaps frequently—in order to get off the roller-coaster of emotions those stressful circumstances create.

STEP #3: ASK GOD TO HEAL YOU AND HELP YOU

This may sound like an obvious step, but over the years, I've realized that many people frantically turn to everybody and every institution *but* God when a crisis hits. They are frantic and scattered in their search for a quick fix.

It is vital that you consciously and intentionally recognize that:

Only God can completely fix you.

Only God can truly heal you.

Only God can thoroughly deliver you.

He may use people to minister to you, but they can never be God.

He wants to act on your behalf, but He has given you the gift of free will, and He will not violate that. You must invite God to fix you, heal you, and deliver you. When you invite Him to do His work in you, He will. That's His promise (see 1 John 1:9 and Psalm 50:15)!

The Word of God tells us that we often don't have what we need because we don't ask (see James 4:2). So . . . *ask!*

STEP #4: ASSESS WHAT YOU HAVE LOST

It's difficult to be objective when you are hurting. I often say to people, "Take a big breath and take one giant step backward so you can see the tree instead of the bugs crawling out from under the bark."

Imagine for a moment that you've been riding a motorbike through a forest on an off-road path when suddenly you hit a big bump, your motorbike goes flying through the air, and you find yourself hugging a tree with your bike in a heap below you. The air has been knocked out of you. You are in shock. But you know this: *I'm alive. I wouldn't be feeling so much pain and shock if I weren't alive!*

Your first step is to unwrap yourself from the tree and sit down for a few minutes to get your lungs working and your nerves calmed down. Then you need to sit up and look around.

What happened?

What's the damage—to me, to others, and to the world around me?

What do I need to do first?

When you take an emotional hit, which is very often linked to some form of material or tangible hit, the same questions apply.

What happened? What's the damage? What do I need to do first?

Do what you need to do in the immediate "acute phase." But then step back, calm yourself, and evaluate what has happened, is happening, and may happen.

STEP #5: MAKE A LIST OF POSITIVE OPTIONS

No matter how great the loss or how dire the circumstances surrounding it, there's always something you can do to move away from the negative and toward the positive. There's always room for faith. There's always room for hope.

I recently heard about a woman who was diagnosed with cancer. This woman had never been seriously ill in her life. In fact, she rarely even experienced the common cold. The idea that she had cancer was virtually unthinkable! She said, "I felt as if the air had been knocked out of me. After the doctor left his consulting room, I doubled over as if I had been hit in the stomach. A flood of questions began to fill my mind, all the way from 'Why me?' to 'What now?' to 'How do I tell my children?' to 'Will I die?' to 'When might I die?'"

She then said, "I finally realized that I was thinking about questions I couldn't answer in that hour. What I did need to answer was the question my doctor had asked me, 'Can you meet with the oncologist this week?' It was already Wednesday. I had to come up with a way of clearing my schedule so I could say yes. The first and most basic thing I needed to do was make an appointment. I focused on the question I could answer, and it gave me the strength to get up out of the chair and walk out of my doctor's office to the counter where future appointments were made."

The next thing this woman did absolutely demonstrates the right course of action for anyone to take when facing a loss or potential loss. She said, "I went home and took out a notepad and wrote down at the top of the first page the words 'Positive Options.' I started making a list. And then I made a decision that I was going to find a way of asking myself questions that I could answer with a positive 'yes.' I started a second list on another notepad. I labeled it 'Yes Questions.'"

Some of the options this woman put at the top of her "Positive Options" list were:

- Call everybody I know who believes in prayer and have them pray for me.
- See the oncologist my doctor recommended.
- Go online to learn as much about my situation as possible.
- Call a nutritionist who can help me fight for my health.

Some of the questions she began to ask herself on her "Yes Questions" list were:

- Is there a good possibility I can beat this? (She had Stage I cancer, so the answer was truly "yes!")
- Does God have a plan for my life? (Always!)
- Does God love me? (Always!)
- Do other people love me? Will they support me in this? (This woman had a very loving husband and children, who were filled with faith and were very supportive. The answer to both questions was a big "yes!")

I don't know what type of loss you may be facing, but I do know that you can benefit greatly from doing what this woman did. Make a list of "Positive Options." Make a list of "Yes Questions." Focus your faith and your activity on doing what can lead you to healing, restoration, wholeness, and recovery.

"But is this really wise and objective?" you may be asking. "Aren't you living in denial by not facing the potential downside?"

"Denial" is saying that something bad isn't happening or hasn't happened. If you are making lists about something, it has already happened and you know it! It isn't denial to focus on the positives.

In choosing to focus on the positive questions, you are setting yourself up mentally and emotionally to follow through on the "yes" answer. You are activating your mind and faith to pursue the positive.

What you think you can do, you will do.

What you think you can't do, you won't even try to do.

If the loss you are facing is a divorce or a death, you may find yourself asking, "Can I ever love again?" That's a question every person can answer with a "yes." Don't ask, "Will I fall in love and get married again?" Nobody can answer that question with one-hundred-percent assurance. But can you love again? Absolutely. It may be a foster child, an older person in the retirement center, or a needy person you meet at the shelter where you choose to volunteer. There are any number of people you can love again. Divorce and death do not take away your ability to love. Your challenge is to find new and healthy ways of expressing love to those who need your love!

The more you see that you have options, and the more positive questions you seek to pursue, the more you are likely to conclude at some point, "This isn't as bad as I originally thought it might be."

How many times have you asked a child, or perhaps were asked when you were a child, "What do you want to be when you grow up?" A child generally can think of a hundred things she might like to be, and often changes her mind from one day to the next. Children "try on" various careers in their minds and in their play long before they face any real career or life-direction choices.

So, what do you want to be when you grow up? The question is still a valid one. It's valid every day of your life! Many people, however, have lost the ability to think of a hundred things they might still like to try, experience, or explore. What about you? Make a list of ten things off the top of your head that you'd like to experience, try, or most beneficial of all, *become*.

I recently heard about a forty-year-old woman who decided to take ballet classes. It didn't matter to her that she was twenty pounds overweight, nor did it matter to her that she was five-feet-four-inches tall and would never be a ballerina in a professional sense. She took classes because she had always wanted to. Good for her!

I also heard about a man who had always wanted to be a teacher, but had entered the corporate world instead. At age sixty, he felt unfulfilled, and his thoughts turned back to his early childhood dreams of being a teacher. He decided to volunteer as a teacher's aide one morning a week in a school near his office. He was high enough on the corporate ladder that he could adjust his schedule to do this. He soon found that those were the most rewarding hours of his week. Good for him!

STEP #6: RECALL THE HAPPY TIMES

Think back to a time and situation when:

- *Something made you laugh*—even if it was as simple as the antics of a puppy, or a child, or a child playing with a puppy!
- *Something warmed your heart*—perhaps a time with family or friends
- *Something made you excited*—perhaps the start of a new project about which you felt great enthusiasm
- *Something made you feel truly "alive"*—something that put a kick in your step and gave you great energy
- *Something pleased all of your senses*—perhaps a walk in the park just after an April shower
- *Something felt holy*—when you truly felt you were connecting with God

- *Something made you feel competent*—perhaps even a game you were good at playing as a child, or a basic skill that you know you can do well any place, any time
- *Something made you feel rewarded and cherished*—a time when you were appreciated, honored, recognized, or made to feel valuable
- *Something was celebratory*—perhaps a party in your honor or a special holiday memory

Breathe those memories into your being. Focus on them. Cradle them in your mind. Let them plant in you a renewed desire to dream, create, and hope. Project those wonderful times from the past into your future. See yourself experiencing those things again.

Those memories may very well be the seeds you eventually plant for your future happiness.

STEP #7: IMMERSE YOURSELF IN GOD'S WORD

When you have taken a serious hit or experienced a major loss in your life, you need an outside source of inspiration. That inspiration is the key to envisioning a brighter future, a better life, a better dream, a better goal, a better relationship. I certainly recommend the Word of God as that source of inspiration. The Word of God not only inspires but also reveals. It is that revelation that brings transformation.

The Bible says that if you meditate on the Word, speak the Word, and do the Word, you will have success (see Joshua 1:8). Let me tell you a little more about that word "meditate." I'm not at all referring to some type of yoga exercise. Meditation in the Bible combines two critical concepts: "to see" and "to mutter."

Begin to "See" a Better Future

The first purpose for reading the Bible is to see a better future for yourself. It is to start envisioning what you might do in your life, who you might become, and what you might accomplish.

The Bible contains countless stories about people who were down but not out—people who touched bottom but were elevated to the top. Concentrate your reading on some of those accounts. Allow yourself to believe that what God has done for others in the past, He can and will do for you.

God saw Ruth, a young woman with a dysfunctional past, gleaning in the field . . . but He also saw Boaz, a "kinsman redeemer," standing at the edge of the field, watching Ruth (see Ruth 2:1–17).

God saw the Israelites struggling to make bricks without straw in their slavery . . . but He also saw the day when they would walk across the dry riverbed of the Jordan River and lay claim to a land of their own (see Exodus 5:7 and Joshua 3:14–17).

God saw Joseph in a pit, where he had been put by his jealous brothers . . . but God also saw the day when Joseph would be the second most powerful man in all of Egypt (see Genesis 37:23–24 and Genesis 41:41–43).

God saw Esther in the humble beginnings of her Jewish home . . . but God also saw her living in a palace as the queen of the land, able to exert influence to save her people from a death sentence (see Esther 2:5–7 and Esther 5:7).

God sees more about you than your past or present. He sees your future! Ask God to give you a glimpse of what He sees you doing and being in your tomorrow.

Get into your Bible and read it as if your life depends on it. The true success of your life on this earth, and your future in eternity, depends on your knowing and believing God's Word, and especially His plan of forgiveness and mercy and purpose for you. Make it a goal to read the entire Word of God, and to read it on a daily basis. It's food for your spirit.

Begin to "Speak" a Better Future

"Muttering" is voicing repeatedly, even quietly to yourself, those things that you are choosing to become, based upon the Word of God. I have been to Israel a number of times, and I have seen many Orthodox Jews walking through the narrow streets of the Old City of Jerusalem, seemingly talking to themselves. In truth, these men are reciting words of the Torah from that morning's readings. They are implanting, memorizing, and internalizing the Word of God. They are fixing their minds on things that are both eternally sublime and earthly practical. They are fixing in their minds' eyes the ideal ways to live their lives.

We are wise to do the same. Read the Bible aloud to yourself. Memorize key verses that have special significance or meaning to you. Seek to implant the Word of God in your mind. "Mutter" its truths to yourself, especially those truths that directly relate to what God says is part of your nature as a Christian.

Speak about the *you* that you will *be*. Speak about the things you desire to *do*. Speak a better future to your own two ears. You'll also be speaking this future to your heart and mind.

Build Up Your Faith

Reading and speaking the Word of God builds up your faith. As your faith grows, you will find yourself being challenged to make changes in the way you think and respond to life. You will feel empowered to do all that God commands you to do in the Word. And perhaps most important, you will grow in your ability to trust God to guide you into a brighter future.

STEP #8: RECOMMIT YOURSELF TO GOD

Jesus once encountered a woman at a well that was outside the city limits. In the course of their conversation, this woman admitted to Jesus that she had had five husbands, and the man with whom she was currently living was not her husband (see John 4:5–42). This woman, like many, continued to repeat poor choices without ever getting to the root of the problem. She was a woman who looked for love in all the wrong places, and probably with all the wrong motives. She no doubt thought that if she just changed the packaging, she could change the person inside and eventually find someone who could meet her emotional needs. She was like a person who keeps drinking poison in the hope that it will turn into medicine.

Jesus gave this woman an option. He said to her, "I can give you what will truly satisfy the thirst inside you." Now, Jesus was sitting by a well, and no doubt used that well as a ready-made metaphor for the truth He was about to impart to her. But He wasn't referring to physical water. He was talking about the inner emotional needs of her life—feelings of anxiety, lack, need, and desire. Jesus asked this woman for a drink of water that would meet a very temporary need in His life. In exchange, He offered her a means of fulfilling her innermost needs in a way that was permanent, even extending into eternity (see John 4:5–42).

Jesus challenged this woman to confront Who she was worshiping. But the woman was much more concerned about *where* she worshiped. Isn't that true today as well? People often talk about their church and their denomination far more openly than they talk about their relationship with God.

The word *worship* means "to give homage to as divine," but it also means "to serve." Worship is expressed verbally, but also in deeds. Jesus told the woman at the well that those who worship God do so "in spirit and in truth" (John 4:23). They worship through what they believe, and also through what they say and do. Worship is very practical. It involves our highest praise, but also our greatest service.

How does this relate to your needs and how you meet them? Simply this: *who* you worship is *who* you will expect to meet your needs, and therefore, *who* you will serve with your greatest devotion. Many people today worship people and entities other than God. Sometimes they worship members of their own families—a spouse, a child, or a parent. People may not call their devoted service "worship," but if push comes to shove, they will sacrifice just about anything they have and are to stay in relationship with the person they worship, succeed in that job they worship, live in that dream house they worship, keep driving that car they worship, gain the favor of that parent they worship, keep that child they worship from leaving home, and so forth. Sometimes the object of their worship is a career, a philosophy, a particular church or denomination, an institution, or a "state of being." They will put the needs of that person or entity above everything else when it comes to the allocation of their time and resources—and they will do so expecting that person or entity to meet their emotional needs fully.

I never encourage people to study false religions or false gods, but even the broadest overview of false worship reveals that people today worship:

- *Fertility gods.* Some women today place their entire identity in motherhood, and they will do virtually anything to bear a child and control the child they bear. They worship at the altar of motherhood.
- *Provision gods.* In the ancient world especially, women looked to a spouse to provide security and sustenance—food, shelter, clothing. Some women today place their entire identity in being married—in having and keeping a husband who provides.
- *Power gods.* Some women today place their entire identity in "liberation," and subsequently "control." They will do virtually anything to be able to manipulate or control a situation—in their families, in their places of work, in their communities. They worship the idea of being in charge.

Ultimately, false gods fail to provide what their worshipers desire for them to provide. Worship of these false gods always fails to satisfy. Not every woman is able to conceive or bear a child, and even if a woman does have a child, that child eventually grows up and leaves home. Not every woman marries, and not every husband is capable of providing. Some husbands die. Not every effort results in the desired outcome. Not every plan succeeds; not every attempt to control works.

Only God can do what He promises to do. Only God does what He says He will do. Only God can meet all needs. Only God can give us an identity that is true, and that lasts eternally.

Jesus made it very plain in His teachings that we are to love God with our whole heart, mind, soul, and strength. And then we are to love others *as* we love ourselves (see Luke 10:27). In other words, we love God and worship Him above all others. Then, we love and serve our own needs so that we *can* give and help others. We are *never* to elevate another person to a position equal to or higher than God, nor are we to elevate that person to a position that negates the value we place on ourselves (see Matthew 22:37–40).

When you are struggling to recover from a loss, ask yourself:

- Who am I worshiping as the source that will meet all my needs?
- Who am I serving with my highest devotion?
- Was I worshiping that person or that entity that I lost?

In the Bible, the prophet Samuel wept over the failure of King Saul. Saul was the only king Samuel knew. We also weep over the loss of the only life we have known. We weep over the loss of the only home we've had, the only love we've experienced, the only accomplishment we've achieved. Weeping is normal. But the day came when God said to Samuel, "Dry your tears and go anoint a new person to be king" (see 1 Samuel 1).

God may be asking you to prepare for a new relationship, one that is of His design and choosing. Stop weeping, get your eye makeup repaired, and prepare yourself for the one He is preparing for you!

In the Bible, the prophet Elijah found himself at a remote brook, where ravens brought him morsels of bread and meat each morning and evening. He drank from the brook. But then the brook dried up and the ravens quit coming. The Lord told Elijah to get up and go to Zarephath, a town many miles away in a place that was foreign to Elijah (see 1 Kings 17). You may have come to a place where your source of provision has dried up. Now may be the time when God is asking you to get up and go to a place that He will show you, or to do things in a different way according to His plan. Get up and get moving!

God has countless ways to meet your needs. Ask Him to show you the *best* way He desires for you to live so He can bless you in the *best* ways.

Shake Off Painful Memories, Worries, Fears, and Failures

13

HEAL YOUR EMOTIONAL PAIN

$\mathcal{T}$he statistics of today's culture are staggering. According to the National Coalition Against Domestic Violence, "1 in 4 women will experience domestic violence during her lifetime. In 2001, 20% of violent crime against women was intimate partner violence. . . . 3 in 4 women over age eighteen who reported being raped were physically assaulted by a current or former husband, cohabitating partner, or date." In response to these and other heartbreaking realities, women are increasingly running for their lives to shelters, many with their children.

The vast majority of abused women do not understand why the men in their lives abuse them. There seems to be no way to predict what will set off the rage that produces flying fists. There's no logical reason for why a person might suddenly flip out and shoot an innocent child, or slash a pregnant woman and toss her body into the ocean. The truth is, no behavior on the part of the woman is necessary. The rage or psychological problem lies inside the abuser and is triggered by something that activates a belief of flee or fight—and he chooses to fight. His target is often the woman nearest to him.

In contrast to many men, women tend to store up memories of abuse instead of lashing out. Women bind the memories of those hurts to their innermost soul. They feel the pain of past emotional wounds for years. Those wounds—often wounds they don't even recognize consciously—affect the victims in a variety of ways.

Certainly men are also abused, but the statistics related to the abuse they experience as boys and adults is not as readily available, perhaps because men talk less about the abuse they have experienced, or process it differently. Whatever the exact percentage for males or females, we know that even one victim is one too many.

All people have some degree of emotional pain, and if they truly want to move in freedom toward a brighter future, they must confront their innermost pain.

GET TO THE ROOT OF YOUR EMOTIONAL PAIN

You need to probe to the deep seat of your emotional pain, not to relive those memories or remain stuck in them, but to bring forth healthy change and to reverse the damage done by wounding events in your past. I often say, "You cannot conquer what you don't confront, and you cannot confront what you don't identify." Ask yourself the following questions:

- Do I frequently feel anxious?
- Do I frequently feel sad?
- Do I frequently feel deeply fearful?
- Do I frequently feel hurt or rejected, left out or unwanted?
- Do I have haunting dreams that cause me to awaken in terror or sorrow?

If the answer to any of those questions is yes, then ask, "Why?" You may have stuffed traumatic acts of abuse so deep within you that you can barely bring them to your conscious mind. You must bring them up, however, in order to be cleansed of them.

Dig deep. Think back over your life. Can you recall the first time you had those feelings? Can you recall any time in your early childhood when you had those feelings?

Write down all of the facts that you can recall about the disturbing event that first made you feel anxious, fearful, rejected, or hurt. Ask the questions a journalist would ask: who, what, when, where, why, how.

What did you come to believe as a result of that event?

Why does a particular environment or situation trigger this habitual pain in you?

What is it that people don't know about you? What don't you want them to discover?

What do you routinely feel, think, or fantasize about in relation to that past pain?

Then describe how you think other people might describe you if they knew all that you've been through, fantasized about, or done. Limit yourself to twenty words.

Before you become too discouraged by what you have written, let me share the good news. Nine times out of ten, what a person writes down is not what other people would really say about her. It certainly is not what God would write about her!

You may think others see you as unclean. God sees you as clean on the basis of the shed blood of Jesus.

You may think others see you as deserving to be punished. God sees you as blameless.

You may think others see you as bad. God calls you beloved.

You may think others consider you a victim. God says you will be victorious.

The Bible tells us to walk by faith, not by sight (see 2 Corinthians 5:7). Simply put, faith is the Word of God. It is God's perspective and His final decision for you. In contrast, sight means "view" and is often expressed as opinion. The command is to walk, or live, by what God has to say about you, not by the opinions of man.

The devil will use many different vessels to whisper accusations in your ear and try to convince you that you have no worth, are unlovable, and can never succeed at being what God has created you to be. But when you are aware of the lie, you can be stronger in refuting it when the enemy of your soul whispers that accusation. Begin now to arm yourself with rebuttals based upon the Word of God.

Relationship with God is easy. It is not something you can earn or even ever deserve. It is simply received on the basis of accepting God's plan of salvation. If you have accepted Jesus as your Savior—if you believe that He is the Son of God who died on your behalf so that you would not need to die in sin—then God sees you through the image of Christ. The Bible tells us that God sees you as

- Totally accepted
- Justified by faith
- In right standing with Himself
- Forgiven
- Beloved
- Free of sins (no longer guilty of missing the mark)
- The recipient of grace
- Empowered and victorious
- Fully accepted among the community of all believers around the world (see Ephesians 1, Romans 4:4–8)

You have the challenge of seeing yourself the way God sees you. This is critically important for you to hear:

As you see yourself, so others will see you.

I am a firm believer in writing down what you believe about yourself. Who are you in Christ? Write it down! Put it in your own words.

Circle what you wrote down, and next to it write in bold letters: TRUTH!

CHOOSE TO LIVE FREE OF GUILT AND SHAME

There is no sin in feeling emotional pain. There is no error involved, no fault. The danger, however, is that emotional pain can cause us to behave—in words or deeds—in ways that do nothing to heal our pain and everything to reinforce it.

How can you reverse this trend? As soon as you feel emotional pain, say to yourself, "Stop! Think!" You may need to say those words aloud. Catch yourself! Identify the pain. Wake up to what is happening. Don't *react* to the situation or to the pain—rather, *respond* to it in a positive way.

Ask God to help you think in new ways, to feel new feelings. Ask God to fill you with His presence so that you will not react in anger, fear, worry, or doubt, but rather, with His love, joy, peace, patience, kindness, and mercy.

Perhaps the most positive thing you can do is to invite Jesus into that painful moment of the past. He can heal every place you have been hurt.

INVITE JESUS TO GO WITH YOU TO YOUR PAINFUL PAST

Sometimes when a person has been abused, injured, or rejected, that person's ability to dream shrivels and dies. Hope is nearly impossible. It's as if something inside the traumatized person shuts down and remains dormant. A resurrection is necessary.

The Bible tells a story about three friends of Jesus: Martha, Mary, and Lazarus. Lazarus died, and by the time Jesus arrived at their home, Lazarus's body had been buried and Lazarus's sisters were in deep mourning. Their emotions were scattered; they were confused, angry, and sorrowful. Jesus said to Martha, the oldest of the siblings, "Where have you laid him?" (John 11:34 NIV).

Jesus did not ask Martha to tell Him about Lazarus's illness, death, or burial. He said, "Show me."

Jesus says the same thing to the person who has experienced death in part of her soul: "Show me." This means in a very practical sense that we need to do two things. First, we need to recall the most painful experience of our life as vividly as possible, with as many details as possible. To do this is emotionally painful. It's scary. In many cases, the feelings associated with the memory are just as real in the memory as they were during the initial experience. God does not ask this of a wounded person so that He might wound that person further. Rather, God asks the person to revisit that scene in his or her memory so He might heal that memory. How? The Bible says that we are to "cast down" every imagination that is not in alignment with God's highest and best for our lives (see 2 Corinthians 10:5). We cast down the horrible memory in our life by inviting Jesus into the scene.

The second step to take is this: see Jesus as being part of the scene in which you experienced deep emotional pain. Put Him into the picture. And then put Him into motion.

When I was only five years old, my father died. My father was my world. He was my primary caregiver, the one who woke me up and dressed me in the mornings, played with me, took me with him as he went about his business, and he was the one who was always looking for the next fun thing for me to explore, learn, or do. The last memory I have of my father is when he walked out of our home in great anger. A short time later, he committed suicide. I was devastated. The wound in me was deep and wide, and went to the very core of my being.

When I revisited that memory and invited Jesus to enter the scene, I pictured Jesus walking in the door of our home. He held out His arms to me, inviting me to come to Him. I did. In my mind's eye, I ran to Him and He picked me up and cuddled me in His arms. I felt His love.

Every time I had a searing memory of my father's death after that, I quickly moved to revisit my new memory of Jesus holding me and loving me. It was the vision of Jesus's love for me that healed me of that emotional pain.

My father's death had created the emotional pain of abandonment and rejection. When I allowed the presence of God to go to the painful place in my heart, I saw that I was not alone, but was held by the arms of a loving God who would never forsake or leave me. That new mental picture changed me. Remember, feelings follow thoughts. When I saw my situation differently, I began the process of transformation. I stopped believing I was alone or undesirable. All behavior stems from belief. When you get to the root of a problem, you can make the corrective adjustments and replace lies with truth, error with correction. A faulty belief system produces a faulty life. A firm, truthful belief system produces a healthy, whole life.

Later in my childhood, after my father's death, I was left in the care of some people who had been very violated themselves. I was often locked in a bedroom closet, left alone in the dark to cry myself into exhaustion, and I was sexually abused on numerous occasions. When I went through the healing process later in life, I invited Jesus into those scenes. He came and sat with me in the dark, holding me and telling me wonderful stories about His time on earth—how the people responded to His healing miracles and the joy He felt when people believed in Him. He gave His light to the darkness. He smoothed my hair and dried my tears and stayed with me until the door of the closet opened and He walked with me back into the bedroom.

Every time I had a painful memory of those abusive times, I quickly moved to revisit my new memory of time spent with Jesus. It was the visual image of Jesus's care for me that healed me of my painful past.

I don't know the pain you may have felt in the past. I don't know when part of you died. But I do know this: if you invite Jesus to that memory—if you *show* Him that scene and invite Him to enter it—He will give you a *now* word for your past pain. His *now* word to you will be one of healing and restoration. He will revive the part of you that died in that old memory.

> God has a now word for your past pain.

Take Jesus to the place where your heart was broken.

Take Him to the place where the crime or trespass against you was committed.

Take Him to the place where you sat in abandonment after being rejected.

Take Him to the place where you heard the stinging criticism that cut you to the core.

Allow Him to be with you and to heal you.

The Bible tells us that Jesus is the same yesterday, today, and forever (see Hebrews 13:8). God is omnipresent. He is outside of time. He is just as real in the past as He is today. In like manner, He is just as real in your past memory as He is in your present thinking and feeling.

Jesus desires to rewrite the script of your life with *Him* as the star on center stage. He desires to rewrite the script of your life so that it's not about human failure, but divine success.

GIVE YOURSELF PERMISSION TO CRY

We cry when we hurt, but what we often fail to recognize is that God is using our tears to flush out the "old" from our lives and prepare us for the new thing He has ahead for us. Tears are part of the healing process. Just as pure water is helpful to the cleansing of an open wound on the body, so our tears are intended to cleanse us of emotional wounds deep within. Cry, and cry freely. But in your tears, listen for God's voice. Listen for what He speaks to you about your future, and about where you are to go next, what you are to do next, and with whom.

REJECT REGRET AND SELF-PITY

Don't wallow in memories of the past. Choose to forget the words of criticism that were aimed at you, or the cutting remark that was made about you. Don't replay those words over and over in your mind. Instead, choose to think about times in which you know you did well or experienced words of praise or encouragement. Choose to focus your thought life on those things that are challenging, positive, and worthy. Take charge over your memories and your thought life. Immerse yourself fully in a new venture, a new dream, a new opportunity.

You may never forget fully what has happened to you in the past, but you can live without painful memories haunting you all night and dogging your steps all day. Don't spend your time with "what-ifs."

Refuse to wallow in self-pity. Nothing is accomplished by living in a memory.

Don't rehash or recycle old memories that are rooted in "if only" thinking. If you continually rehearse old thoughts about what might have been, what could have been, or what should have been, you'll become discouraged and very likely won't do anything to improve your own situation. Your discouragement today will become the "what if" and "if only" state that you dwell upon tomorrow.

Regret is one of the worst emotions a person can feel.

If you are genuinely sorry for something you have said or done in the past, including what you perceive to be a lost opportunity, take that to God. Ask Him to forgive you, to teach you what you should learn from that experience, and then to help you build upon what you have learned to create a brighter tomorrow.

Your relationship may have ended. Ask God to forgive you for your part in its failure, show you what not to repeat in your future, and then prepare you for what He has next for you.

Your business or job may have ended. Ask God to forgive you for anything you did that may have caused the business to fail or the job to be terminated and to show you what not to do in the future. Then ask Him to show you what to do next.

In any area of loss, failure, or change, ask God to renew you from the inside out, to remake and remold you, and to prepare you for all that He has in your future. The truth is, your future is brighter than your brightest past! There's nothing so dark that God's light can't shine into it. There's nothing so bad that God can't forgive it. There's no pit so deep that God can't lift you out of it, dust you off and clean you up, and send you down the road toward a good goal.

> The truth is, your future is brighter than your brightest past!

TURN YOUR FACE TOWARD YOUR FUTURE

Yesterday is in the tomb.

Today is in the womb.

What you are intimate with today is what you will birth tomorrow. What you think about and dream about in the secret place of your own heart is what will give birth to your future words and behavior.

Choose to focus on those things that will nurture and nourish you. It is those things that will give you the faith, courage, and creativity for your future.

There's nothing you can do to change your past. You can, however, have a serious impact on designing your future.

14

TAKE THE RISK AND TRY AGAIN

*W*hen you have experienced failure or abuse or have been full of worry, often the last thing you want to do is to take a risk, embrace change, or "try again." Those, however, are the very things you *need* to do and *must* do if you are truly to live an authentic life from the inside out.

You were not created for fear. You were not created to be shackled by negative emotions or memories. You were created to live out a bold, dynamic, creative life filled with expressions of love and joy!

There are six things you can do to bolster your courage. Take these steps!

#1: QUIT DWELLING ON PAST FAILURES

Faults and failures are a part of life. Accept that fact, and when you fail, pick yourself up and choose to move forward. You haven't really failed unless you refuse to get up! At the same time, recognize that others around you also have faults and fail from time to time. Don't get stuck in those moments, either your failures or theirs.

I've met people who are far less judgmental of others than they are of themselves. Give yourself permission to be human and to err. Every person makes mistakes. Every person sins. We all fall short of the glorious potential God has placed inside us (see Romans 3:23).

I'm not at all advocating that you settle for mediocrity, or that you deny your mistakes or blame others for them. Rather, recognize your mistakes, take responsibility for them, and choose to pursue greater excellence.

Failure is part of life's learning process. God created that process, and he intends for you to *learn* from your failures so that your life continually moves in an upward pattern.

Some things in your life you learned to do very quickly, and if you hadn't learned them, you wouldn't be here right now. For example, you learned to breathe on your own seconds after you were born. You learned to suckle a bottle or your mother's breast. You learned to cry to get your needs met.

When my son Brad began learning to eat with a spoon, he insisted that he feed himself. It took ten times longer for Brad to feed himself, and he made quite a mess, but I let him do what he wanted to do because I knew he needed to learn that skill. Learning can be messy. It can take time.

When you learned to walk, you fell down repeatedly. But you kept getting up and trying again.

We learn through success, through failure, through repetition, through trial and error. And what is true in physical growth and development is generally true in every other area of life. The good news is that God never says to us in our toddler emotional state, "You stupid child. You are a total failure because you fell down. Don't ever try to walk toward me again." *No!* A thousand times, *no!* God reaches out to us in the same way I reached out to my son and said, "Come on, honey, come to mama, take another step, now take another. Come to mama's open arms."

God never calls you a failure when you fall. So don't call yourself a failure. Learn from your mistakes and move on.

#2: IDENTIFY THE RISK WORTH TAKING

Taking a risk may mean returning to a dream that has been delayed or deferred. In some cases, it means trusting God to plant a new dream in your heart.

In other cases, the risk may involve reconciliation of a broken relationship—taking a chance at starting over. Or the risk may mean walking away from a broken relationship and starting anew with a different person.

In all cases, the risk of trying again involves brushing yourself off after an unsuccessful attempt and actually doing something that pushes you toward your future. Don't just *think* about trying again. Don't just *talk* about it. Take action!

Learn what you can from your failure and apply what you learn to a new, fresh start.

I once heard of a man who owned a major national newspaper in the United States. While he had been extremely successful, his greatest concern was that his sons had not experienced failure yet, and he feared they would not handle it well. He had personally attempted to establish a new independent newspaper when he was in high school, and it had failed. He had failed in his attempts to establish a new newspaper when he was in college, and again shortly after he got out of college. Each time, he learned important lessons, and eventually he did establish a national newspaper that has now been wildly successful for decades.

A number of very well-known, successful people experienced serious failures in their lives. They, too, chose to learn from their shortcomings and apply what they learned in order to succeed.

No one goes through life without failure. What we often don't recognize, however, is that failure can be a friend.

Colonel Sanders had a string of failures in several business fields before—at an age when most men are retiring—he founded Kentucky Fried Chicken.

S. Truett Cathy experienced a variety of failures before he founded Chick-fil-A.

Thomas Edison documented hundreds of failures before he invented a light bulb that worked.

Abraham Lincoln lost more elections than he won, but he eventually won the presidency of the United States.

Start with a Small Risk

I realized not long ago that my entire adult life, I've worn either red or pink nail polish on my toenails. I like red. I like pink. But I also like a lot of other colors. Why hadn't I worn them? There was no good reason I could come up with! One day I decided to try white polish . . . and then a very pale pink . . . and then vampire-deep crimson. How daring of me! Especially since I wore closed-toed shoes the first few times I wore those untried colors.

You may be laughing, but in actuality, this was a daring move for me. It might have been similar to a very conservatively dressed man daring to wear a new color of shirt, or an outlandish tie. I'm glad I took the risk of trying something new! Deep inside, I knew that this wasn't an important area related to my character or my purpose on the earth—it was a matter of style. And when it came to style, I had at different periods in my life let others dictate my choices, rather than basing my choices on what I liked and preferred.

I decorated rooms in our home to suit what others would like, to accommodate *them*.

I chose which automobile to drive based on what I thought others would like to ride in.

I wore clothes I thought others would find appropriate on me.

That was the old Paula.

The new Paula decorates in her own preferred colors and style. She wears what she enjoys wearing. She drives what she likes to drive. And she invites others to get to know her a little better in the process.

The truth is, when you base decisions about style upon what truly is pleasing to *you*, you are revealing yourself to others in a new way. You are taking the risk of revealing the authentic you to the world. And nine times out of ten, who you are *will* be acceptable and, even more than acceptable, valued. When you reflect your authentic self to others, they have a freedom to honestly reflect themselves back to you.

> When you reflect your authentic self to others, they have a freedom to honestly reflect themselves back to you.

What about the ten percent of people who might not accept the real you? You may need to explore the reason for that. Is the other person upset that he or she no longer controls you in this area of style or decision-making? Is the other person jealous? Does the other person feel threatened by the compliments that you receive? Those questions are worthy of exploration, but in asking them, be prepared to discover where you might be challenged to grow, or in some cases, to grow up!

#3: MONITOR YOUR ATTITUDE AS YOU TAKE A RISK

Make sure you are building your future without guilt, without vengeance, and with gratitude.

Without guilt. Guilt and shame can be like a dark cloud over your head and over any new venture you undertake. Guilt can cause you to hesitate or second-guess a new relationship or venture. The result can be a failure to grasp the opportunities that come your way.

Guilt creates feelings of unworthiness, and if you do not value yourself, others won't value you either. You will not attract people who can help you succeed—rather, you will attract people who will drag you down and perhaps even entice you into behavior that adds to your guilt. Ask God to forgive you for any part you may have had in failed relationships or loss. Then accept His forgiveness and forgive yourself (see 1 John 1:9).

Without vengeance. A vengeful, angry spirit can destroy anything you attempt to establish. People will sense your anger and withdraw from you. Nobody wants to do business with, start a romance with, or develop a friendship with a vengeful, angry, or bitter person. Choose to forgive those who may have offended or rejected you in the past, and start a new chapter of your life free of bitterness.

Don't retaliate or seek to show someone how good you can be. Choose to show yourself and the world at large how good you already know you are because you are connected to a good God! If you proceed with a vengeful spirit, you will shackle your past to your future. The weight of old pain can drag down or halt your forward motion. Letting go of your anger and feelings of vengeance can give you great emotional energy—well-directed to a better and brighter future!

With gratitude. Move forward in your life with thanksgiving that you are alive to see a new day.

Those things that *should* have destroyed you . . . haven't.

Those things that *should* have killed you . . . didn't.

Those things that *should* have made you weaker have actually made you stronger, because you survived them.

Voice your thanksgiving to God for seeing you through your loss.

Generously thank others for their part in helping you. People respond enthusiastically to those who are thankful for their advice, financial assistance, practical support, and prayers. Give thanks, and you will reap a harvest of help.

Be grateful for what *remains* in your life. I often tell people who are going through a loss, "People never fully appreciate what they have and who they are until they experience loss." Put the focus on what you *have,* not on what you have lost. You still have so much! In fact, you have far more than whatever amount you lost.

#4: DRAW HOPE FROM HOW GOD HAS HELPED OTHERS

In addition to what you read in God's Word, choose to take hope from the way you see God working in the lives of other people. I am one-hundred-percent confident that there is at least one other person on this planet—and very likely in your immediate circle of family, friends, or fellow church members—who has been through what you are going through right now. We tend to think that our problems and needs are unique and isolated—that nobody has experienced either the scope of the problem or the depth of the pain that we are experiencing—but in truth, all needs and problems are common to the general human condition.

The same is true for the things that tempt us to doubt God or lose hope. The Bible states it this way: "There hath no temptation taken you but such as is common to man: but God is faithful, who will not suffer you to be tempted above that ye are able; but will with the temptation also make a way to escape, that ye may be able to bear it" (1 Corinthians 10:13). We tend to think that temptation involves sexual sin, greed, or taking in harmful substances, but this verse in the Bible is actually tucked between verses that deal with pride and idolatry. Anything that entices you to give in to the ways of the flesh, rather than pursue the things of God, is a temptation, a drawing away.

The good news is that God provides a way out of temptation. He provides avenues for renewing our faith in God, our hope in the future He has planned for us, and for our commitment to obeying Him. How do we best come to understand that other people have been through what we are experiencing, and that they have emerged from the experience stronger and better, not destroyed or defeated? By listening to the stories of other people.

You can learn a great deal from the example of others. Discover how God has worked in them and through them. Discover what they have done to renew their faith and keep their eyes on the goal. Discover how they maintain their hope even in what seem to be hopeless and devastating events.

Learn how other people discipline themselves to reach their goals.

#5: KEEP AN EYE OUT FOR NEW OPPORTUNITIES AND NEW METHODS

God will send you opportunities. Don't miss them.

God may be designing a new method just for you. Be open to it!

Don't get stuck in a preconception that God is going to answer your petitions in precisely the way you envision. God has thousands of methods He can use to bring into your life the things He wants you to possess. He has infinite options for bringing about the accomplishment of the goals He calls you to pursue.

Sometimes, we simply fail to open our eyes to what others around us may see as obvious in our situation.

I recently heard about a young man who had a very rare condition linked to an uncommon birth defect. The only known medical cure for this ailment involved surgery, which was successful in the vast majority of cases, without any need for follow-up medications or treatment. Amazingly, one of the few surgeons in the nation who performed this rare surgery moved to the city where this man lived and set up practice less than a mile from the man's home. This surgeon is considered one of two or three international experts on this condition. The young man initially took a firm stance: "God is going to heal me." He later acknowledged that God, indeed, had sent exactly what he needed in the form of an expert surgeon right in his neighborhood. This surgeon was God's provision for him. He had the surgery, the outcome was successful, and his recovery is complete.

Certainly, having surgery is never fun. This young man no doubt wished for God to alter the birth defect inside his body without any help from the medical world. God, however, sometimes uses medicine as a method of healing for us.

Why share this in a book about living an authentic life by God's design? Because the methods God will use to help you bring your self-concept and character in line with His plan are varied. God certainly uses your consistent reading of His Word to teach, admonish, correct, and challenge you. He may use this book as a method to help you discover your authentic self, and I pray that He will. God may use a sermon you hear next Sunday, the story you hear at a dinner party next week, a televised documentary, a recurring dream or vision, the wise words of a psychologist or counselor, your grandmother's diary, a long conversation with a parent, or any one of a thousand other methods to show you ways in which you need to change your thinking, change your responses and behaviors, or change what you are hoping and dreaming will happen in your future.

Don't limit God when it comes to how He will answer your prayers or help you to make the changes that He desires to see in you.

Expect New Opportunities with Each New Day

Awaken each morning expecting a wonderful opportunity to renew your life.

It's a day to think new thoughts.

It's a day to feel new feelings.

It's a day to explore new options.

Choose to look at a new day as a new opportunity for you to experience God's faithfulness, love, and compassion.

Expect to be renewed and transformed just a little bit more into the likeness of Christ Jesus.

#6: EMPTY YOUR MIND OF WORRY EVERY NIGHT

I strongly recommend that every night you empty your mind of all the day's worries. The Bible tells us to cast all our cares on the Lord (see 1 Peter 5:7). See yourself doing this. Take a physical action that symbolizes this truth to yourself. Turn your head over on your pillow and imagine that all tension, anxiety, worries, fears, and troubling moments of criticism and failure are flowing out of your mind and onto your pillow. Then fluff the pillow, roll over, and prepare for a peaceful night's sleep. Ask the Lord to give you the "sweet sleep" that He promises to those who allow God's wisdom to replace their fears (see Proverbs 3:24).

Everyone sleeps, but they don't all awaken refreshed or fully rested. Often, even when the body is resting, the soul is not—it is a bundle of anxieties, insecurities, and fears. The mind races, trying to resolve the issues of the day. The habit of emptying your mind each night is a real key to developing a pattern of sleep that produces both genuine rest for the body and rest for the soul.

The person who experiences a night of sweet sleep carries that feeling of rest—often described as peace or serenity—with him throughout the next day.

An amazing upward spiral begins to form.

Those who are serene on the inside often find that life flows much more smoothly on the outside. There's no full explanation for how and why this happens, but those who have deep calm in their souls generally find that things around them break less often, they have fewer accidents, people treat them with greater civility and favor, they make better choices, they are more open to hearing about and pursuing good opportunities, and their relationships are more loving and helpful.

The more peaceful a day, the less anxiety there is to empty at night. The sweeter the sleep, the more peaceful the following day. And so forth. A life of peace begins to be established.

The Role of Prayer and Meditation

The Bible tells us that we are to cast all of our cares to God in prayer, by making our requests known to God with an attitude of thanksgiving (see Philippians 4:6). Then, as we do that, God acts. He imparts His peace. Our part is to voice our thanks to Him and to cast our cares onto Him. We are to request what we need and then trust Him to meet our needs. His part is to provide all that is beneficial for our eternal good and to give us a dose of divine peace.

God's peace transforms how we think. It enables us to answer calamity with calm reason and understanding, to see order in the chaos, and to know the best direction to pursue. It releases us to walk with divine revelation and insight, almost as if we have a secret map for the way out of the problems that arise.

God's peace transforms how we feel. We answer fears with faith. We have an ability to speak with measured voice and without feeling threatened or frantic. We are able to give strength to others, rather than collapse into a puddle of weakness. We respond with assurance that not all is lost and there is much to be gained. We experience God's presence with us, and His presence is an ally that is more powerful than any foe.

God's peace allows us to function to the maximum of our ability and beyond. It allows us to function in the ability that God imparts.

That's authentic living!

15

ACCEPT CHANGE AS GOOD

$\mathcal{E}$verything in life changes. If you don't learn the art of transition, you may not be flexible enough to bend through the curves of life. When change comes, we often worry that things won't be the same. We fear that change will bring yet another opportunity for failure. We are creatures of habit, and we don't want our boat rocked by change.

Many people I encounter do not see change as positive, primarily because it is unfamiliar. But the truth about change is this:

- Life moves on whether you like it or not. Change is inevitable.
- You can influence change.
- You can have a significant role in designing a future that is vastly improved over your past.

Choose to develop a master strategy for managing change so that it is *good*. There are at least four things you need to consider as you make change work in your favor.

#1: DON'T LIMIT THE STREAMS OF INPUT IN YOUR LIFE

Don't limit the streams of good information and godly wisdom in your life. Read widely, seek multiple opinions, have numerous conversations with a broad spectrum of people. Avail yourself of experiences that will help you reach your godly dreams and goals.

When it comes to finances, I often advise people, "Don't rely on just one stream of income." There's added security and protection in having multiple sources of income.

When it comes to emotional input, there's added emotional security and protection in having more than one source of love in your life. Your love basket should be filled in many different ways—the love of your spouse, children, family members, and friends.

#2: DETERMINE WHAT YOU DON'T WANT TO REPEAT

As you strategize about changes in your life, you must become very analytical about what you have lost. That is the key to not repeating past mistakes. It's the key to creating a future that is better than the past.

Ask: What don't I want to do again?

I have encountered countless women during the last two decades of ministry who were mourning the loss of relationships, and in the vast majority of cases, they were mourning the loss of men who weren't good to them or for them! In some cases, the relationships they were mourning had been marked by emotional or physical abuse, not only of the women but of their children. Let me assure you that God has something better for you if you are in a relationship that is marked by abuse! There's a person out there who is much better suited for the real you. You deserve to be cherished, appreciated, and loved. You are valuable, unique, and precious. You really are all that!

I have also met people who mourned the loss of jobs they hated. Yet they had been doing work that they found unfulfilling, without challenge or opportunity to grow, and without adequate recognition or reward. What a miserable way to live!

Early in my life, I knew that I was not cut out for a nine-to-five job in an office cubicle. I was certainly willing to work long hours—and on many days, my job is five-to-nine, and by that I mean five in the morning to nine at night. What I couldn't imagine was being confined to one small space doing one limited set of tasks. I set myself to find work that had many facets and involved encounters with many people. What I found was a life of full-time ministry, and nothing in my imagination could be more fulfilling to me and to the way I desire to spend my time and talents. I moved to Florida with my husband, Randy, and began ministering in the poorest part of Tampa.

Let me assure you of this: if you get involved in helping the poor who live in inner-city projects, you are going to find work that has many facets and many people. Every day, I encountered literally hundreds of people, each of whom had different needs and sometimes very different personalities. I encountered dozens of different tasks, from reading to young children, to talking to businesses about donating food and supplies, to sharing Bible lessons and financial advice with welfare mothers, to praying for those who had spiritual needs. I found a job that suited the real me.

I have met a number of people who have lost their homes. After all, I do live in hurricane-prone Florida. In many cases, the loss has been partial, and in some cases, the loss has been total. One woman said to me after her home was destroyed, "We're going to rebuild, but this time, we're going to build a house that has the walls and windows where I want them!"

She was committed to building on the same foundation that remained after the storm, but she planned to build a new structure according to a very different house plan. Not only was she putting walls and windows where *she* wanted them, but she was planning a different look for the exterior of the house. And not only that! She described for me some of the things she would do to make her new home safer and easier to maintain. All of her efforts were being directed toward something better. How I admire that attitude! She is building a home that suits the real her.

If you have lost a relationship, you may have been freed from a relationship that was harmful to you emotionally, spiritually, or even physically.

If you have lost your job, you may have been freed from work that didn't truly fit you.

If you have lost a possession, you may have been freed to pursue an even better possession that requires less effort to maintain.

The truth is that some losses are for your personal *good*.

Ask yourself:

> The truth is that some losses are for your personal good.

- Did this person or thing that I lost make me feel worthy, important, or significant?
- Did it provide me with a degree of emotional stability and security?
- Did it give me an opportunity to learn, take on challenges, and grow as a person?
- Did it give me genuine love, affirmation, and recognition?
- Did it allow me sufficient opportunities to take responsibility for my own life?

If the answer to any one of these questions is "no," identify what you need to do to ensure that your future will be better.

When my son Brad was young, I often said to him when he misbehaved, "That isn't working for you." I wanted him to learn that behavior had consequences and that he could control his own behavior. He could determine what he wanted as a goal, and then do the things necessary to reach that goal.

Be brutally honest with yourself about what didn't work for you in the past, or what isn't working for you now. Don't repeat those behaviors! Don't make those same unproductive, unrewarding, unsatisfying choices.

#3: TARGET AREAS FOR POSITIVE CHANGE

Don't attempt to change everything at once. Target specific areas where change might create a situation that is more productive and satisfying.

First, evaluate specific habits, memberships, relationships, and tasks or chores. I encourage you to take four pieces of paper and label each page with one of these words: Habits, Memberships, Relationships, and Tasks/Chores. Then list your key habits, your memberships, important relationships, and key chores or tasks that you do routinely.

Next to each item, note whether or not the item or relationship is "productive." By "productive," I mean that it produces "good output"—a lot is being done, growth is evident, and results are having a beneficial impact on all involved. Also note whether or not the item or relationship is satisfying. By "satisfying," I mean purposeful and fulfilling.

For anything you identify as less than highly productive and satisfying, ask, "What do I need to change?" These areas that are unsatisfying and unproductive are where positive change can be maximized. What do you have to lose? How much worse are you willing to let things get?

If you keep doing what you've always done, you'll likely keep getting the results you've always had. If a habit or routine in the past isn't working for you, if a relationship isn't growing or satisfying, if a method isn't producing good results, shift it into the "to be changed" category of your life. One of the definitions of insanity is doing what you've always done and expecting different results.

#4: SEEK TO IMPROVE RELATIONSHIPS

Relationships can always be improved in some way. I strongly encourage you to adopt the CAN plan:

C = Communicate Your Feelings

Begin by communicating your feelings to yourself. Identify what you feel and how intensely you feel. Give voice to your feelings if you have someone who will listen to you without judgment, in total confidence, and with wise counsel. Write down your feelings. In communicating your feelings, and especially when you put them into writing, you are doing two things. First, you are claiming or validating the feelings as your own. Second, you are releasing them from your memory. Your mind says to itself, "I don't need to remember all that. The words are written down in a way that can be remembered without me. I can move on to other thoughts." The signal goes to the heart, "You are free to move on to other feelings." In writing down your feelings, therefore, you are freeing both your mind and heart to move on to new thoughts and new feelings, which in turn will give rise to new behaviors.

When you know what you are truly feeling, express those feelings to the person who has hurt you (if there is a continued relationship). Let them know that their actions, intentional or unintentional, caused you pain. Don't accuse them of anything. Simply state how their behavior made you feel. While addressing them, take ownership of your feelings rather than placing all responsibility on their behavior.

A = Assert What You Would Like

Identify for yourself what you would like to see happen in the future. You may simply know that you want something different, without knowing quite what that would mean. Write down what you would *like* to feel—joy, freedom, peace. Identify new behaviors that will move you toward your desired goal.

Many people don't understand the true role of feelings. They think they must *feel* before they *act*. But actions can create feelings. If you don't feel joy, smile anyway. You can't smile for very long before you genuinely begin to feel more joyful. If you don't feel love for another person, give something of yourself away that is positive and helpful to that person. You can't give in a positive way for very long before you start to feel more love toward that person.

N = Negotiate the Best Steps for Resolving Your Differences

You and the other person may not have the same feelings or even the same perspective on the situation. You and the other person may differ on what you think future behavior should be. You can't have everything your way or have everything you'd like! Negotiate. Life is full of give-and-take compromises with other people. As long as God's boundaries are not crossed, there's room for such compromise and negotiation.

Let me give you a couple of dialogues as examples:

DIALOGUE #1: STICKING TOGETHER

SHE: I feel frustrated when you wander off and ignore me at parties.

HE: Can we compromise on this? I don't see why we should "stick together" at a party. We can gather so much more information if we go our separate ways and then talk it all over later.

SHE: How about if we agree to stick together for the first ten minutes of the party and hook up for a few minutes together periodically—at least that will send a clear message that we are *together* at the party.

HE: Agreed.

DIALOGUE #2: OVERSPENT BUDGET

SHE: I feel angry when I watch all my expenses very carefully all month and then discover that you've purchased a new pair of expensive golf shoes.

HE: But I need new golf shoes.

SHE: I want us to make a budget each month that we both agree we'll stick with.

HE: Okay, but I want to build some "mad money" into that so we can each buy some things without consulting the other person.

SHE: I agree. How about a spending limit of $100 for each of us as "mad money" each month? If we want to buy something that costs more than $100, we consult the other person.

Do you see how this can work? By identifying your feelings, you are not accusing another person of ill motives or blaming another person for causing your feelings. You are owning your own feelings. In stating what you would like to see happen, you are moving on from the past and giving direction to the future. In negotiating, you are recognizing and validating the feelings of the other person.

The result? Healthy resolution of conflicts. Improved communication. A relationship that is better.

AT ALL TIMES: REMAIN POSITIVE ABOUT CHANGE

One of the reasons that people don't change is because they don't believe change is possible.

As a child I was amazed when I went to a circus and saw elephants tethered to the ground by very small stakes. I couldn't understand why the elephants didn't break free and wander away. Later, I learned the reason. When a baby elephant is first being trained, it is staked to great logs or trees. It may struggle greatly, pulling against the rope or chain that ties it to the log, but after repeated failures, it eventually gives up. The young elephant concludes that when a rope or chain is around its foot, it *cannot* be free. Even a small stake can hold the elephant in its place once it has reached that conclusion.

How many people are in exactly that same situation emotionally or spiritually? They believe that they are forever bound to a bad situation or to a bad outcome. They have been conditioned by past experiences to conclude that nothing good can or will happen. They don't take any risks in testing the boundaries of what *might* be, because they've already convinced themselves about what *will* be.

Are you a prisoner to your past?

Are you chained to something mentally, when in fact you are free to make new choices and decisions?

Believe that you can change.

Believe that change can benefit you.

> Believe that you can change. Believe that change can benefit you.

Activate Your Faith

Believe that God desires positive change for you and that He will help you make good changes.

The Bible tells us that our faith is *pleasing* to God (see Hebrews 11:6). That doesn't mean that God likes us better if we have faith. It means that our faith allows God to work fully in our lives, and therefore, our faith brings about God's "pleasure" because He can bless us to a far greater extent.

God knows that faith is what produces real change—first in our thinking, and then in our speaking and acting. And as we speak and act in faith, faith will produce change in others around us and in the prevailing circumstances of our lives. Our faith is pleasing to God because it aligns us with what He desires for our lives.

When you change beliefs, you change behavior . . . and in many cases, when you choose to change the habits of behavior, you also impact and solidify beliefs. Beliefs and behavior are inseparably intertwined. If a person says he believes one thing and does another, he is false, both to himself and others. Behavior always reveals what a person *really* believes, regardless of what that person might say. If you look at the fruit in a person's life, you will be able to identify the roots.

Choose to believe what you believe to be God's very best, and then pursue the best. In the end, you will change your life not only for the better, but for the best!

Take Control over What You Think, Say, and Believe

16

TAKE CONTROL OF THE
WAY YOU THINK

*I*t's said that we each think about sixty thousand thoughts a day. And nobody is responsible for those thoughts other than the person thinking them.

You control what you think about.

And you control how you act on your own ideas.

You may be influenced by the words and actions of others, or by the environment around you, but what you choose to do with a thought is entirely up to you.

The apostle Paul gave some very clear instructions to the first-century Christian church about thoughts (see Philippians 4:4–12). He advised them that there were five things they needed to do in order to have peace, and each of those things involved their thought life in some way:

Rejoice always. This means to give thanks and praise continually, in all circumstances. To give thanks and praise in all situations does not mean that you are necessarily overjoyed by the situation itself. It means, rather, that you choose to respond to even the most negative situation in a positive way, thanking God and others for their help and provision, praising God for who He is, and encouraging others with a positive attitude and affirming words.

Live in moderation. A peace-filled life requires balance—in what we eat and drink, how much we sleep and exercise, how tightly we schedule our days, how we balance work and play, how we balance alone-time and people-time, and all other practical areas of input and output. A life of moderation doesn't happen by accident—it requires intentional choices. It requires thinking about what you do before you act. It requires making plans and following through on them. It requires making choices for health and sticking with them.

Turn all of your concerns into prayer. Go to God any time you have a problem, need, nagging question, or pressing decision. Go to God with choices big and small. Go to God when you are frustrated, angry, or hurt. Don't worry—pray! Worry doesn't solve anything, but prayer can move mountains (see Matthew 17:20). Prayer is vital to turn negative thoughts into positive faith.

Choose to dwell on thoughts that are true, honest, just, pure, lovely, things of good report, things of virtue, and things that are praiseworthy. Take charge of what you ponder, talk about, and remember. Look for the positive side of a situation or person and set your mental energies in that direction.

Choose to follow the examples of godly people. Do what you have learned, received, or heard from people who live whole, stress-free, God-honoring lives. Reflect on those you admire the most and ask yourself, "What about that person's life is attractive to me?" Think about who would be a good mentor, role model, or teacher for you, and approach that person.

The New Testament was first written in the Greek language, and the Greek word for "think" in Paul's writings refers to "taking an inventory or making an estimate." Take an inventory of your thought life. Estimate how much time you spend thinking about a particular issue, person, topic, or situation in a day. What captivates your thinking?

I strongly encourage you to list at least five things that you believe qualify as "good thoughts" in each of the following categories:

- Truth
- Honesty
- Justice
- Purity
- Beauty
- Positive Report
- Virtue
- Praiseworthiness

Did you have trouble coming up with five things for each category? If so, spend some time thinking about why.

In order to think positive thoughts, you need positive input. You need to expose yourself to things that are honorable, beautiful, and godly. If you do, those very traits will begin to characterize you as a person.

If you look at garbage long enough, your mind will become a cesspool. Weigh carefully what you read and what you watch—the images that you put into your mind. Weigh carefully what you listen to—the lyrics of the songs you hear, the programs you tune into. If you listen to angry messages long enough, you can't help but feel anger deep within.

Most worries and fears involve things that never come to pass. Take inventory of your worries, anxieties, frustrations, and fears. Then choose *not* to think worrisome, anxious, frustrated, or fearful thoughts.

Some people don't believe that a person can choose how he thinks. I'm here to tell you that you *can* choose your thoughts. Even if you have thought a particular way about something for decades, you can still change your mind. You do not need to remain stuck in an old way of thinking.

> You do not need to remain stuck in an old way of thinking.

TAKE YOUR THINKING TO HIGHER LEVELS

Do you remember the children's story that begins, "Pussycat, pussycat, where have you been?" The tale relates how a cat went to see the queen, and when it was asked later about the experience, the only thing the cat recalled was that it had seen a mouse under the queen's throne room chair. Very often, we tend to look at one incident, one conversation, one embarrassing moment, one failure, or one aspect of a situation and focus on that to the exclusion of the whole. One fragment of life—limited in time and in space—does not represent the whole.

Let me say it again: What you focus on the most becomes strongest in your mind. If you concentrate most of your thinking on what is upsetting to you, you will eventually lose sight of other things that are rewarding, encouraging, or uplifting.

Look at a problem from all angles. Look at people from many vantage points. See their strengths as well as their weaknesses.

Every person has flaws, but if you think only of that person's flaws, you will lose sight of his good points. The truth is, every person has a good side—even if it's dormant, buried, or not yet realized.

If you concentrate only on another person's negative qualities, you will eventually come to dislike or perhaps even despise that person. But that isn't all. You will also find that your attitude in general begins a downward spiral. You may think you are seeing only the negatives of that one person, but you are actually developing a perspective of negativity that will extend to other people and to yourself. It's a little like putting on sunglasses. You may put on sunglasses to take the glare off the water as you are cruising along in a boat, but once you put the sunglasses on, the entire world is a little darker. If you wear those sunglasses into a dimly lit restaurant, you may think night has fallen!

Choose to see the positive traits in other people and in various situations, and you'll find it much easier to see the positive in yourself and to feel hope.

People who regularly dwell on negative thoughts are significantly less content than others. They may think they are being realistic by focusing on the negative, but in truth, they are creating negativity in their own emotions that will eat away at their peace.

A PROCESS OF ONGOING RENEWAL

The Bible speaks of a renewing process for our minds (see Romans 12:2). That word *renew* in the Greek actually refers to renovation. It implies that there is an out-with-the-old, in-with-the-new process. The Bible reinforces this concept in other places, speaking about people "putting off the old behaviors" in order to "put on the new behavior," or "discarding the old identity" in order to "take on the new identity" (see Ephesians 4:24, Colossians 3:10).

There is a formula for renewed thinking. In essence, it's a formula for reprogramming your mental habits. "Is this brainwashing?" you might ask. In truth, most people need some washing of their brains so that they will think purer and nobler thoughts! The formula is this:

READING THE WORD OF GOD CONSISTENTLY + FOCUSING ON CHANGING OLD NEGATIVE MENTAL HABITS INTO NEW POSITIVE ONES + TIME + FAITH = RENEWED THINKING

Let's break it down:

Read the Word consistently. You must feed your mind and heart truthful ideas on a daily basis. God gives us the instruction and inspiration we need as we read the Word of God daily. His instruction and inspiration are like the manna that was given to the Israelites for nearly forty years when they wandered about in the wilderness between Egypt and Israel (see Exodus 16:35). The manna came in sufficient quantity for each day, with nothing to spare. God was building *trust* into His people. He wanted them to depend on Him to meet their needs every day. He does the same today. He gives us what we need when we need it, so that we will learn to trust Him in all things at all times.

The Bible challenges us to plant the Word of God in our hearts so that it dwells therein (see 1 John 3:24). In the Greek language, *dwell* refers to homesteading and abiding. The Word resides in us. Homesteading doesn't happen by accident. A person must choose to homestead a particular parcel of ground and to remain on the land. In like manner, we must read the Word of God and determine that we are going to remember it, apply it to our personal lives, and obey it. Make a decision to read the Word of God daily.

Consistently focus on your thinking. Guard your thoughts. Choose which problems to concentrate on, and what ideas to consider. Choose to discard any idea or fantasy that contradicts what you intuitively know to be good and pure.

Allow sufficient time. Recognize that the cleansing of your mind is like water flowing over rocks in a river. Over time, the rocks' jagged edges become smooth. Over time, God renews and refines your thinking.

Have faith. You must *believe* that you can change the way you think and that God will help you in the process. The Bible says that when we ask God for something, we must believe that we are going to receive what we desire—and that includes receiving the ability to establish a new and godly set of mental habits. Unless you believe, you don't receive. When you do believe, you do receive. That's not my principle—that's God's principle (see Mark 11:24).

Choose to live by what God's Word says, regardless of how you feel. God's Word doesn't change. Its principles are fixed and applicable to all people of all ages in all nations at all times. Your faith must become as constant as God's Word is unchanging.

Ultimately, faith is far stronger than any mood you may have. Moods change, and emotions can be like a roller coaster. Faith is intended to be steadfast and unwavering (see Ephesians 6:13).

There's no telling what might be accomplished if your faith is hooked up to an unchanging God and is based upon God's unchanging Word!

Every person needs some degree of renewal. No matter how good your behavior, how pure your thoughts and motives, or how much your life aligns with God's Word, there's always room for more change, more development, and more improvement. You will never be fully perfected—but you can put yourself in a position to experience greater and greater perfection, which means there is continual room for growth and expansion. Ask God to do His work in you. He renovates in a way that brings about our best future.

17

REINFORCE YOUR THOUGHTS BY WHAT YOU SAY

*T*houghts give rise to spoken words. The process is so automatic that many of us find ourselves thinking, *Did I say that?* We are surprised that our mouth speaks before our minds fully engage. Sometimes the words just come flying out of us, for good or for bad.

The Word of God encourages us to give expression to our noblest and highest thoughts. One of the best confirmations to yourself that you truly believe God's Word is to hear yourself *speaking* God's Word spontaneously in response to life situations. Speaking God's Word is also how we encourage and motivate ourselves. It's how we activate our faith. The Word of God encourages us to sing songs to ourselves, including "new songs" (see Psalm 40:3 and Psalm 96:1). We are to give voice to our thanksgiving and praise.

We are wise to give positive affirmation to ourselves. Never expect another person to say to you what you aren't saying to yourself. You are the first and foremost compliment-giver and inspirational speaker in your life!

Do you catch a glimpse of yourself in the mirror and say, "Hey, good-lookin'?" Why not? Even if you aren't looking your best that day, you can still affirm yourself, "Hey, gal! You're better looking than you're looking right now, and tomorrow's a new day."

Do you finish the big project at work in record-breaking time and in a way that has "excellence" written all over it? Applaud yourself. Give yourself a "way to go" speech. Tell yourself that you've done well. Do you pull off the unexpected? Pat yourself on the back. Recognize that you've done a good thing.

It's never wrong to remind yourself of your strengths, your identity in Christ, your good deeds, or your positive contribution to your family, friends, community, or church.

If you're like me, you have probably heard a lot of negative talk over the years. We all have people who drop us or disappoint us. The Bible records the story of a young man named Mephibosheth (see 2 Samuel 4:4 and 2 Samuel 9:10–14). He was the grandson of Israel's first king, Saul. His father was Jonathan, the heir apparent to the throne. After Saul and Jonathan were killed, a nurse picked up young Mephibosheth and ran to what she perceived to be a safe place. But Mephibosheth fell, and his fall left him crippled. The nurse simply wasn't strong enough to carry him.

People in your life may not have been strong enough to carry you either, or to give you the love and affirmation you needed. Ultimately, only God is strong enough to carry you all the time, in all situations, and to a place of unchanging security. Trust Him to do so.

Rather than replay old tapes of the *negative* things that have been said to you, start making new tapes of *positive* statements. I'm not talking about literal recordings. I'm talking about "tapes" we play in our minds. Create new ones. Speak about your strengths, your talents, your successes. Speak about the good things you've done and the good motives of your heart. Speak about the good character you are developing and the virtues you are displaying.

You may ask, "Is this pride?"

No. Pride is comparative. Pride is rooted in saying that you are *better* than someone else or that you have done *more* than someone else. Positive self-talk simply tells the story of you. It doesn't compare.

Does this mean that you should never talk to yourself about a mistake? No. It does mean that when you are discussing a mistake with yourself, you should separate the mistake from your core identity. You *make* mistakes, but you never *are* a mistake.

Many people are their own worst critics. I like this play on words: "A person's worst enemy is his or her inner-me." Evaluate your work, but do so in a way that applauds what you have done well. Never discount the good that you have done. Never second-guess those things you have done with good intentions. Trust God to work out any misunderstandings about your good deeds or intentions. He can sway the perspective of another person in ways you aren't able to.

Laugh at yourself. But don't laugh in a derisive tone of voice. You will do stupid things in life that are genuinely funny. But you aren't a joke. Laugh at your behavior, not at your character or identity.

I was looking at one of my old journals recently, and I decided to read aloud from it. I burst out laughing—at myself! Most people who see me only on a platform or on television have no idea what a quirky sense of humor I have. I like it when I can amuse myself by my own words.

SELF-TALK CAN MAKE A POSITIVE DIFFERENCE

Can self-talk make a difference? Absolutely! If you make self-degrading remarks, they have likely been dragging you down for years, even if those remarks were made under your breath or only in your thoughts. Affirmations will build you up!

I often talk to myself when I'm running. I speak to my legs, "Come on, girls; you can do this! You can finish this lap. You're strong. You're beautiful. You have what it takes. You can get me home!" The more I speak, the stronger I feel.

I have a friend who talks to herself when she goes to a cafeteria for lunch. She speaks to herself, "You may have only enough to be satisfied, and it will be something healthy. I know you can limit yourself to a salad or salmon. You have the willpower to do this. You are a successful healthy eater and you can resist all temptation on this food aisle. You can choose iced tea instead of a sugar-based drink. Conquer this cafeteria line." She says, "I talk to myself until I'm at the cash register. It works!"

Do such affirmations produce new behaviors and habits? They don't hurt, and they certainly can help! You can talk yourself into your own best choices and decisions. You can talk yourself into your best behavior.

If you don't feel quite right about speaking such positive things over your own life, then read aloud God's Word. I recommend Romans 8:37, 1 John 4:4, and Philippians 4:13.

TAKE A BOW—ACCEPT THE COMPLIMENTS

When others compliment you, accept their affirmations. Don't discount them.

When you hear applause, take a bow.

If you respond to a compliment by saying, "I don't deserve that," you are telling the person who gave the compliment that he or she made a mistake. You are also telling yourself that you are unworthy. The truth is that the other person was right and you *are* worthy.

Say, "Thank you." Or even better, "Thank you very much!"

When you accept a compliment, you send a signal to yourself that you agree with the person's positive assessment. You affirm yourself. Self-affirmation is one of the most positive habits you can adopt.

Speak in the first person. Tell yourself who you are and who you are becoming in Christ. Write down your self-affirmations. Here's a set of affirming statements I once wrote in my journal:

MY AFFIRMATIONS TO MYSELF

I am trusting God.
I am believing that God's promises are coming to pass.
I am blessed.
I am valuable.
I am beautiful.
I am strong.

I am smart.

I am okay.

I am walking in the light of God's truth today.

REMIND YOURSELF OF GOD'S DESIRE TO BLESS YOU

Speak words of truth to yourself:

God wants you to have good health—the best health you can have, not only in the physical, but also in the emotional and spiritual realms.

God wants you to have good relationships—family and friends who will love you and value you.

God wants you to have peace in your heart—calm assurance that He will protect you and provide for you in personal and eternal ways. God will create for you a place where you and He can live together forever (see John 14:1–4). Such peace cannot be taken away from you by any person or any situation.

God wants you to know His forgiveness and to experience His presence and power. He wants you to have an abiding relationship with Him.

WRITE TO YOURSELF ABOUT YOURSELF

In addition to speaking positive things to yourself about yourself, write an occasional poem or letter to yourself. My private journals are sprinkled with these. I don't consider myself to be a poet *per se,* but my writings do speak to my heart in positive ways. The poems that flow from your heart will speak to you as well, and no other reader is necessary but *you.* Here's a sample of one of my "poems to Paula" in a journal from long ago:

> *Not so long ago—*
> *a tenderness robbed,*
> *an innocence stolen—*
> *How will you see*
> *the world now?*

Shattered, torn?
Hopeful, adorning?
A view for you to see—
determined by your focus—
With eyes full of tears?
Wounded and full of fears?
Or enlightened by all
your experience that
spanned over this year?
Your choice.

I am mine—
Only mine am I—
Responsible for the choices I make
and the way I choose to see.
No other to care for
the wellness of my soul—
Nor to mend the deep pit
and dark black hole.
It is you that must care, love,
and protect—
At all costs, never to neglect.
For you are yours
And only yours are you.

SPEAK ADMONITIONS AND DECLARATIONS TO YOURSELF

Just as you speak and write affirmations to yourself, admonish yourself too. To admonish is to advise, usually in a mild but earnest way. At times, to admonish is to *insist.* You may think of admonition as "preaching to yourself." When you admonish yourself, you are preaching what you know you need to hear! Speak to yourself what you know to be the truth of God's Word and His commandments for your benefit.

Here's an entry from my journal from a few months ago:

My Admonishments to Myself

Paula, pick yourself up and give your cares to God! Trust Him today, Paula, and see His promises come to pass.

I admonish you right now, Paula, to believe with all your heart, mind, and soul that you are:

blessed
valuable
beautiful
strong
smart
favored
okay!

Paula, you *will* walk in these truths all day today!

Declare Who You Are!

Declarations can be statements about who you are or who you resolve to become. They can be promises you make to yourself. They can be vows or commitments to yourself. The declaration may include a statement of faith or a prayer. Below is one I made to myself not long ago.

A Declaration to Myself

I declare to myself this day:
To take care of and nurture myself
To find and stay in that place of peace I have discovered
deep within
To never lose the dance in my step
To never lose those distinctive things that separate me
from the masses and that have made me who I am

To never cease to believe that I am great
because of who I am in Christ Jesus.
God, forgive me for allowing anyone or any thing
to become You and rob me of life.
I love You, Lord!

A LOUD "AMEN" FROM HEAVEN

We often say "amen" in church services, meaning, in essence, "I agree with what the preacher is saying." The true meaning of the word, however, is a declaration that we desire what is being said to come to pass. To say "amen" is to say "Let it be so!"

When you declare to yourself the best and highest statements about who you can be in Christ Jesus, when you admonish yourself to obey God with your whole heart, mind, and soul, when you affirm to yourself what God has done for you—all of heaven replies, "Amen!" May it be so! May it come to pass! May it be the reality of your life!

18

CHANGE FAULTY
BELIEF HABITS

*N*ot long ago, I faced a major water-damage disaster in the entry hall in my home. That home repair job taught me a universal set of principles. In most renovations—whether in the material world or in the process of self-discovery—we face a five-step process, which I'll explain later in this chapter.

What does this have to do with your thinking? Some people don't just need a polishing or washing of their minds. They need a massive overhaul of their deepest belief system. They don't just need renewal—they need a serious renovation of their habitual beliefs.

Are you aware that you have habits related to your faith?

Habitual beliefs are deeply engrained in you. They have been reinforced countless times. They are subconscious, for the most part, and seem automatic. Habitual beliefs give rise to spontaneous, impulsive behavior.

Not all habitual beliefs are negative or unfruitful. *Faulty* habitual beliefs, however, can be devastating. They are the ones that need to be replaced if a person truly is going to live an authentic life from the inside out.

Before I explain to you the renovation process, let me tell you how we develop faulty habitual beliefs.

THE ABC PROCESS OF THINKING AND BEHAVING

Even the most minor spontaneous behaviors go through a filtering process in our minds.

A = Activator

Something in the environment triggers an old memory and what has become a habitual way of responding to it. For example, an old song can trigger a memory of a date you had when you were a teenager. If the date was a good one, you may have feelings of happiness and delight. If the date was a lousy one, you may experience feelings of pain, rejection, embarrassment, or even hatred, depending on just why the date was lousy.

B = Belief

All habits carry an element of belief to them. We do some things because we like to do them; we believe them to be good habits. We do some things because we believe we should do them. We don't necessarily like the habit, but we believe it is for our ultimate benefit—for example, eating certain foods, taking certain medications, or exercising. And we do other things because we believe no real justice will be carried out unless we hang on to the memory of it and hold the offending person accountable. In those cases, we tend to cringe inwardly, awaiting the day when justice will be established. These are the beliefs that most often lead to the consequence of emotional pain.

C = Consequence of Emotional Pain

What we believe is what causes us to feel pain, or fear, or dread. The Activator doesn't automatically produce the Consequence. It's the *belief* that triggers the emotional consequence. What happens to you is not nearly as important as what you *believe* about the experience.

I recently heard about a woman who, upon being introduced to the father of her friend, was given a big hug by the man. This woman thought the man was a little over-exuberant, but attached no real belief to the hug. After all, he had just given his own daughter an even bigger hug. She decided her friend's father was a very friendly, warm man, trying to show fatherly affection to her, just as he had his own child. Then she saw the look on her friend's face.

Her friend's eyes were filled with tears, and she was trembling. "What's wrong?" she asked. Her friend said nothing in the moment, but later she admitted that her father had abused her sexually when she was a young teen. She was scared to death of her father, and especially of receiving big hugs from him. She saw those hugs as part of the abuse pattern in the past, and they filled her with terror. She *believed* her father was about to hurt her, and when she saw her father give a similar hug to her friend, she believed her friend might also be hurt. Her belief caused her pain.

One of these women felt no pain because she had no habitual belief of terror or fear associated with a hug. The other woman felt tremendous pain.

We need to keep in mind that what *habitually* makes you angry may not make me angry. What *habitually* frustrates me may not be what frustrates you. What *habitually* causes both of us to be anxious may not be what causes anxiety in a third person. Our responses are individual.

It is the belief that causes us to react to the trigger or activator.

And here's the end result:

Your habitual beliefs produce in you a prevailing self-concept.

If you are habitually fearful, you have probably internalized a self-concept of weakness. You likely have come to see yourself as someone who can easily be abused, defeated, or hurt—and as such, you think you are a person who *deserves* to be abused, defeated, or hurt.

If you are habitually anxious, you have internalized the idea that you have no control over a situation. You likely have come to see yourself as a person who has no power and can be injured by anybody and anything. You may believe at some deep level that you *deserve* to be injured.

If you are habitually sad, you have internalized a self-concept that you don't deserve to be happy or rewarded. You believe at a deep level that you are flawed, faulty, unlovable.

And so it goes. It may not be this clear on a surface level, but if you will objectively and honestly examine your life, associations, and actions, you will discover belief and behavior.

What we come to believe about the people and situations that cause us pain becomes what we believe about ourselves.

You may start out thinking that what another person does to you is hateful. Perhaps they have mocked you or said untrue things about you. But if you do not challenge that behavior in your mind, you can too easily begin to adopt what they say or do and begin to believe that there's an element of truth in their words and actions. You begin to internalize a belief that perhaps you deserve their hurtful, hateful behavior, and over time, you begin to loathe yourself for being so hateful.

Another person's hateful behavior can eventually lead you to hate yourself—even if you did absolutely nothing to deserve that original act of hateful behavior!

"Oh, not me," you may be saying. The truth is that you and all other human beings are prone to this process. The process is emotional, not rational. At its root is a lie that is planted by someone's ungodly words or behavior. It grows in us because we dwell on what happens and give it more thought than we should. It produces lousy fruit—primarily the fruit of a very low self-concept. For example:

A father calls you stupid.
A mother calls you ugly.
A teacher says you have no future.
A coach tells you that you have no talent.
A boyfriend tells you that you are trash.
A girlfriend tells you that you don't fit in.
A group laughs when you come near.

We may be able to shrug off the lie once. But if it is repeated, and from more than one source, we all too often begin to believe that their words or actions are true. And over time, we reinforce that belief into a habit until

> Your habitual beliefs produce a prevailing self-concept.

eventually we see ourselves as stupid, ugly, with no future and no talent, trash, and unworthy of fitting in. We see ourselves as unlovable and without value.

So how do we begin to renovate these very deeply entrenched patterns of thinking and believing? Back to my home-repair renovation!

THE PROCESS OF BELIEF RENOVATION

1. Identify the Root Problems

First, we must identify the core problems that are creating the negative effects in our lives. Now, in the case of the water damage in our home, I obviously could see the water on the floor. The problem was plainly evident. As you consider your ways, you are likely to see the obvious problem behaviors in your life. The challenge is to discover *why* this is being produced. What is the core issue, the *real* problem?

In my case, the air conditioner was leaking and the water was running through a wall and seeping under the floor. I needed to repair the air-conditioning system in order to repair the floor.

In most cases of faulty habitual beliefs, a person has accepted a lie as being true. She doesn't mean to believe a lie, but she does. The more people have lied to you about who you are and what you are capable of being and doing, the more important those people were to you, and the earlier in your life the lies started to mount up, the more prone you are to having bad habitual thinking. Very few people emerge into adulthood unscathed. And if they do, they'll encounter lies as an adult—from people in the workplace, in the marketplace, on the media, in the neighborhood, from their friends.

You may not have been told a direct or obvious lie, but a disconnect between words and actions may have produced a faulty belief system. Maybe you were mistreated or neglected. Maybe someone's body language spoke volumes to you. Any of that, if accepted as truth, can create bad habitual thought patterns.

Not long ago, I saw a fictional scene on television in which one young man said to another, "I'm your friend who tells you that you aren't good enough for the homecoming queen. Who else is going to be that real with you?" Ah, but the truth may be that this young man is *exactly* the type of person the homecoming queen is dreaming about when it comes to long-term character and reliability.

Once lies lodge in the mind, they are difficult to remove, and all too easy to recall. Even small triggers from your environment can unleash a host of negative thoughts and feelings. The mind tends to go on auto-pilot when emotions run deep. The tremendous challenge is to identify and separate lies from truth. Most people have to undo a great deal before they can redo.

2. Pull Up and Discard Whatever Is Bad or Damaged

After the water damage in our house, we had to remove the old flooring. It was a messy process, and because the floor had been put down with such strong adhesives, it took a while.

The old habits—especially the old *thought* habits—associated with your faulty self-perception may take a while to be pulled up and discarded. Nobody has a change of perception overnight. The change can *start* instantly, but a new habit of thinking takes time.

I recommend that you sit down and spend some time making a list of what you need to discard from your life.

Many people find it easiest to start with a "Don't Do" list. Make a "Don't Do" list, identifying behaviors that should not be part of a positive, healthy lifestyle.

Now review that list. Next to each item, put the behavior you *should* do and give a reason *why*.

For example:

DON'T DO LIST	DO HABIT . . . AND WHY
Don't get in a fit of rage.	Control and temper your anger. Make better choices and decisions, and remove yourself from situations that trigger volatile behavior.

DON'T DO LIST	DO HABIT . . . AND WHY
Don't get romantically involved with a person too quickly.	Get to know a person. It takes time for a person's character to be revealed.

Now add to your Do Habit list a decision about your own life and identity that is positive and godly. Here are a couple of examples:

DON'T DO LIST	DO HABIT . . . AND WHY	WHO I AM
Don't get in a fit of rage.	Control and temper your anger. Make better choices and decisions, and remove yourself from situations that trigger volatile behavior.	I am a person in control of my emotional responses, capable of making decisions and choices that will lead to a good future.
Don't get romantically involved with a person too quickly.	Get to know a person. It takes time for a person's character to be revealed.	I will be in relationship with a person of very high character because I am valuable and deserving of mutual respect and honor.

As difficult as it may have been for you to make lists like those above, that's the easy part. The *real* challenge lies in addressing the "Undo List" of bad thought habits. Take time to write down your negative thinking by putting your thoughts in categories according to their importance to you. Don't limit yourself to just one thought in each category. Identify as many negative thoughts as possible. The length of your list is not a mark against you—it is a very positive step toward your knowing what it is that God desires for you. God promises to enable you to make the changes . . . but first, you need to identify the problems!

Below are examples:

A SAMPLE "UNDO LIST" OF THOUGHTS

About God	God is just waiting for me to mess up so He can punish me.
About Church	The church just wants my money.
About the Opposite Sex	(For a woman) No man is capable of being faithful. (For a man) Women are too emotional to be trusted.
About Marriage	A person has to be married to be socially acceptable.
About Work	My job defines my value as a person.
About Family	My estranged child hates me because I am a lousy parent.
About Other People	All rich people are arrogant jerks.
About Myself	I can't make the changes I want to make.

I don't know what your list of thoughts will be, but I can guarantee you this: as you make this list, you will identify things that, deep down inside, you *know* are not the truth! How will you know that? Your spirit will recognize that these thoughts are not in alignment with what you have been reading daily in God's Word. Also, most people, if they get quiet enough and are objective enough, know truth from lies. Dig deep and discover the authentic you. That's the key to a full, satisfying, rich, rewarding life according to God's design.

The Bible says that God gives a measure of faith to every person (see Romans 12:3). God doesn't just design someone and then abandon that person to struggle for the rest of her life. Rather, He expects to help a person discover who she was designed to be, fully believe that she can become that person, and take the steps necessary to grow and develop the traits and skills associated with her destiny.

Struggle and frustration come from living a life that is false, or not designed for you. It's similar to wearing a garment that doesn't fit. You are never really comfortable. But God delights in revealing to you who He designed you to be. He gave you His Word. He gave you a specific set of talents and abilities. You are good at doing at least one thing, and very likely, several things. Chances are, you *like* doing what you are good at. That's your design!

God gives you the ability to believe that you can learn, improve, grow, develop, and become who you were created to be. That's faith.

God gives you the courage to take positive and practical steps toward your fulfillment.

God freely imparts insight, faith, and courage to those who ask Him to do so. If you are lacking in any of these three, ask God to help you!

When you *don't* believe you can succeed, you will have a nagging feeling of frustration deep within. Something will tug at your mind. You'll know that there's something missing, something more, something still possible.

The Bible tells us that every person has an ability to discern basic right from wrong—even a person who has never heard about Jesus (see Romans 1:10–23). When you have a negative thinking habit, if you will spend some time exploring it, there's a very high probability that you will come up with what it is that's faulty about your own thought processes. You will know that something just doesn't ring true about a belief you hold, even one that you've held for a very long time.

A woman said to me not long ago, "All my life I was told I was 'heavy-set.' It's true that I have a large bone structure, but that doesn't mean that I'm automatically destined to be fat. I had to change my self-perception from being 'fat girl' to 'fit girl.'" Her change of self-perception led her to lose sixty pounds during the next year.

Once you have confronted the thoughts that you need to undo, make a list of thoughts you need to turn into positive mental habits. Don't limit yourself to just one thought in each category. Identify all the thoughts you believe you need to turn into new, positive mental habits.

Do you find yourself saying, "I don't know what the right thought should be?" If that's the case, go to God's Word. Use a tool called a concordance to look up various subjects and get God's opinion. For each new thought-habit, write down the Bible verse that tells you this is a good mental habit to develop. Use that list as evidence any time you question whether the new thought-habit is worthy of your time, effort, and concentration.

If you can't seem to find your way in this, go to a godly person who knows God's Word. Ask that person to sit down with you for an hour and help you get started.

The truth is:

- God loves you, desires what is eternally best for you, and has a plan and purpose for your life that will give you fulfillment, joy, and an abiding sense of purpose.
- The church exists for your benefit—to help you grow spiritually and to give you an opportunity to use your talents to help others, and to equip you for the purposes of God and gather you into worship.
- You can have a successful marriage relationship with a person who is faithful and respectful, someone who honors you and with whom you can raise a family or produce "spiritual children"—those who accept Jesus as Savior through your example or teaching, as well as those who are put in a position to learn about God from you.
- You are capable of producing high-quality work, of learning new information and skills, and of working in ways that benefit this world.
- Other people are amazingly like you, regardless of the color of their skin, their nationality, race, or culture. Like you, they need God's forgiveness, have unique talents and abilities, and desire to be loved.
- You can build good family relationships and friendships.
- If another person is unwilling to work with you toward reconciliation, you can forgive that person and entrust him or her to God.
- You are worthy of respect and love. God desires to produce His character traits and virtues in you. You are a one-of-a-kind creation with a one-of-a-kind personality and giftedness, and therefore, with a

one-of-a-kind purpose. You are special beyond measure. If you have received Jesus as your Savior and have received God's forgiveness for your sins, you are destined to live with God forever (see John 3:16).

Don't believe me? Go to God's Word—the irrefutable source of all truth—and you'll discover that I'm sharing the truth with you. This is the real deal!

3. Prepare Yourself for New Changes

Our challenge in our home-repair job was to let the damaged area dry out thoroughly. The contractors we hired told us plainly, "If you don't let this floor dry out completely, you're going to have an even bigger mess with mold and loose flooring." We heeded their warning, set up fans, and gave the floor time to dry completely. The drying process took far longer than we expected. Even though the floor felt dry to the touch, it wasn't thoroughly dry.

As you develop the new thought process associated with an accurate self-perception, you need to prepare yourself correctly. What does this mean in practical terms?

From my perspective, it means that you go to God's Word and immerse yourself in it. You read it, and then read it some more. You underline verses that speak clearly to you. You say to yourself again and again, "This is for me. This applies to my life."

Immediately after I experienced God's forgiveness and was given a Bible, I knew that every answer I would ever need in my life was in that Bible. I don't know exactly *how* I knew that, but I knew it. I held up the Bible and said aloud, "Every answer I need for life is in this book." And then I set myself to find those answers.

I made reading and knowing the Bible my number-one priority. I spent hours each day reading the Bible. I took the Bible into my mind with a ravenous appetite for knowing God's truth. If I got to parts that I didn't understand, I asked people around me who did understand. I asked God to reveal to me what He was saying and how it applied to my life.

I recognized that the way I had been thinking about myself didn't line up with what God said about me, so I began to change the way I thought about myself.

I recognized that the choices and decisions I had been making, and the behaviors I had been displaying, didn't line up with what God said to do, so I began to change the habits of my life.

I began to change the way I treated other people—I had always been friendly toward others and valued other people, but there were other areas in which I could see clearly that the way I approached people and what I expected from others needed to be adjusted. I lined up my communication style and my way of relating to other people with what God said to do.

None of that happened overnight, and it is not completed today. It's an ongoing process of transformation. But I did two things right—I didn't try to force the process, and I didn't allow myself to become discouraged when my life didn't change overnight.

I hadn't arrived at the place where I was overnight. And I didn't see myself arriving at a new destination overnight. I knew enough about fruit production to know that a very fine sapling of a fruit tree still takes time to grow and produce good fruit.

If you know you have been forgiven by God and have a relationship with Him, and if you are intent on seeing yourself as God sees you and becoming the person God has made you to be, then you need to get into God's Word and line up what you believe about yourself with what He says.

Do what God says to do.

Keep believing that God is at work in your life.

Keep declaring that God's Word is true in your life.

Keep believing God's Word and quoting it often to yourself.

> If you know you have been forgiven by God and are intent on seeing yourself as God sees you and becoming the person God has made you to be, then you need to get into God's Word and line up what you believe about yourself with what He says.

4. Install the New and Polish It!

The new flooring in our entryway was installed in a couple of days. We went from a cement foundation to beautiful hardwood flooring, and the transformation was beautiful. The new wood floor, of course, didn't go down fully polished. It was only after it had been installed and after the adhesive had been given time to set that the heavy-duty polishing machines were brought in.

There will come a day when you will look around you and say, "My new life isn't at all what my old life was. God has done a miracle." Expect God to continue to refine you. His polishing will continue for the rest of your life.

5. Continue to Maintain What Has Been Installed

The transformation process in a human being's life is just that—a *process*. There are always cleaning and polishing to do. There's always a need to guard against damage. The good news is that God does that work in us as we continue to trust Him, to read and apply the truth of His Word to our lives, and to make the choices and decisions that He prompts us to make.

Even the person who has a very strong, positive self-perception can become discouraged at times, or feel unworthy or unloved. When those feelings or thoughts come, quickly identify them and consider them to be a brief episode of faulty thinking, not a permanent reality. Don't allow a habit of faulty self-perception to develop. Guard against it. Stay in alignment with what God's Word says. His Word does not change—it is sure and trustworthy.

You *can* change your faulty habitual beliefs. It's work. It takes time. But in the end, the beautiful authentic you shines in a way it never has before!

Establish New Boundaries

19

SET HEALTHY BOUNDARIES

$\mathcal{A}$ friend of mine purchased a lovely home a few years ago in an older, established part of town. The property was bordered on one side by a hedge of tall, thick holly bushes. As the months passed, my friend wondered why the neighbors didn't prune their bushes. And then the day came, as you might suspect, when she looked again at the legal diagram of the property she had purchased and discovered that the hedge of holly was *hers*. The boundary line with her neighbor was just beyond the hedge, and her responsibilities included not only the holly bushes, but also a tree and two small patches of lawn.

Property boundaries determine who owns what, and therefore, who is responsible for what. In a very similar manner, emotional and spiritual boundaries determine identity and responsibility.

Boundaries give us our sense of individuality. Boundaries tell us what is ours and what is not.

At the most basic physical level, your skin is a boundary. It separates you from other people and from the rest of your environment. In countless ways, boundaries keep negative influences—such as germs— out of our being, and keep positive necessities—such as our vital organs, bones, and muscles—within us. Emotional and spiritual boundaries are intended to function in a similar fashion: keeping negative factors out of our psyche and spirit, and positive beliefs, feelings, attitudes, and ideas within our minds and hearts.

WHERE DOES YOUR RESPONSIBILITY END?

You are responsible for setting boundaries for your own life. But responsibility has limitations when it comes to relationships. Only God is fully responsible for His creation of all people, at all times, and in all places—He has delegated partial responsibility to us.

The first two brothers mentioned in the Bible had a serious difference of opinion when it came to how they were to offer their thanks to God. One brother, Abel, brought a thanks offering of a lamb—something he did not produce, but something he valued highly. The other brother, Cain, brought an offering of grain or vegetables from the ground—something he had worked hard to produce, and something about which he was proud. God accepted Abel's offering and rejected Cain's. Cain was livid with anger. Rather than take God up on His offer to change his offering and his attitude, Cain killed Abel in a raging fit of jealousy (see Genesis 4:1–12).

The issue, of course, was not purely with the nature of the sacrifice that each brother brought to God. It was an issue of heart. Abel came with humble awareness that he was utterly dependent upon God for all things at all times, and his offering reflected his belief: "I'm giving to You, God, something You gave to me. The lamb is Yours; I'm Yours; all of creation is Yours. I know that life is symbolized by blood and that without You, God, I have no life."

Cain came with his bundle of produce and asked God to bless his work and honor his efforts. His offering reflected an attitude: "Look what I've done. I produced it; I'm in charge; I'm capable. Life is a matter of rewards and accomplishments and good works, and I expect You to bless my efforts."

The Bible tells us that God "respected" Abel and his offering, and God did not respect Cain and his offering (see Genesis 4:4–5). The word *respect* literally means to regard or to value. Cain's attitude was the opposite of what God valued.

After Cain murdered Abel, God asked Cain, "Where is Abel, your brother?" Certainly God knew the answer—He asked so that Cain might hear his own answer! Cain replied, "I do not know. Am I my brother's keeper?"

In truth, of course, Cain knew where his brother was—he knew the exact spot where his brother had bled to death.

God replied, "What have you done?" (Genesis 4:10 NIV). He wasn't asking—or requiring—that Cain be responsible for his brother from sunup to sundown. God was asking Cain to take responsibility for his actions and his attitudes. God challenged Cain about his anger and required that he own up to the sin he had committed against his brother.

God requires the same of us.

God does not ask or require us to be "on duty" 24/7 when it comes to responsibility for other people. God does not ask or require us to do what only He can do: convict, save, deliver, heal, and make another person whole.

DON'T TAKE ON A ROLE THAT ISN'T YOURS

When we accept responsibility that isn't ours, we in essence take on God's role. We proclaim to ourselves and to God, "I'm capable of changing another person. I'm capable of saving another person, redeeming another person, healing another person, or making another person whole." God says simply, "That's not your job. You can't—I can. Don't try to do what you are not equipped to do. Don't try to accomplish what you are not capable of accomplishing, what you are not equipped to accomplish."

God asked Cain, "What have you done?" Cain's responsibility was linked to a deed. In truth, we are always responsible for what we do. We are responsible for our influence on others—which comes about as a result of our words and deeds—but we are not responsible for what another person does or doesn't do. We are responsible for what we say or write, for the body language that conveys our attitude, and for our public and private behavior. But we are not responsible for how another person responds to our words and deeds.

If someone willfully chooses to misinterpret or to take offense at your words, the accountability for her response lies at her feet.

If someone willfully chooses to ignore you or fight against you or stalk you because of things you have said or done, the responsibility for those behaviors rests with him.

If someone attacks you or abuses you, the responsibility for hurtful behavior is his, not yours.

In like manner, you are answerable for how you respond to another person's words and deeds. The person who erupts at you in anger does not *make* you respond with angry words, a clenched fit, or a pouting silence. Your reaction to another person's anger is *your* responsibility. Before God, you are accountable for *your* response, not the other person's behavior.

> You are accountable for your response, not the other person's behavior.

An old saying often used as an excuse is, "The devil made me do it." The devil didn't make you do it. You chose to do it.

The mean person didn't make you respond as you did. You chose to respond that way.

The unkind stranger didn't force you to react as you did. You made a choice, consciously or subconsciously.

The manipulative or cheating spouse didn't force you to take the action you took. You made a decision with your God-given free will to respond as you did.

RESPONSIBILITY IS COUPLED WITH ACCOUNTABILITY

God did not ask Cain about what Abel had done. He asked Cain, "What have you done?" Responsibility has a flip side called accountability.

Another person may not have the power to hold you accountable for your actions. But God has both the power *and* the interest.

A legal system may not be able to hold your critics or abusers accountable for their actions, but God holds them accountable.

Your social environment may not punish the person who causes you emotional or physical pain. Your social group may not hold your enemy accountable. But God does. He says in His Word, "Vengeance is mine" (Romans 12:19). God has ways of exacting justice that we cannot begin to imagine.

We need to take God's accountability requirements seriously, not only in those situations where we desire for God to exact His vengeance on those who hurt us, but in those situations where we desire God to extend His grace and forgiveness to us when we hurt others.

Matthew 7:3–5 asks us why we are trying to get a speck out of our brother's eye when there is a plank protruding from our own eye. God holds us accountable for our thoughts, words, actions, and behavior, both against Him and against other people. God requires that we take responsibility for our actions. We are accountable to God for what we do. And perhaps most important, the foremost person for whom we are responsible is ourselves.

20

THE ART OF SAYING NO

*O*ne of the most famous characters in musical theater, even though it is a secondary part, is the character of Ado Annie in *Oklahoma!* A flirtatious, eager-to-be-married girl, Ado Annie's most famous line is, "I'm just a girl who cain't say no."

Our world has lots of Ado Annies in it today.

People who can't say no to that extra piece of pie.

People who can't say no to sexual temptation or inebriation.

People who can't say no to helping others at the expense of their own well-being.

People who can't say no to sleeping in on Sunday mornings.

In order to set healthy boundaries, a person must be able to say no. That's the key statement that sets a boundary!

What many people don't realize is that "no" is a complete sentence. You don't need to make up a long excuse or justification for saying no. You don't need to defend your position. Just say no.

For some people, saying no is easy, but for many people it's extremely difficult. How easy is it for *you* to say no?

Many find it easier to say no to a person who is distant from them—a stranger on the phone or a mere acquaintance—than to say no to a person who is close to them, and especially to a person for whom they care deeply or with whom they live or work on a daily basis. The irony is that the people who are most likely to place demands on your time, money, emotions, and talent are the people who are closest to you and, therefore, tend to be the people to whom you are most reluctant to say no. But you *must* say no if you are to maintain a healthy sense of self.

When we say no, we refuse to accept any unwanted demands on our life. We are protecting our innermost being from an intrusion that we discern will be a negative influence on our overall quality of life or our relationship with God.

THE ARTFUL SKILL OF SAYING NO

It takes a certain amount of skill to say no to another person, and like all skills, developing the artful skill of saying no takes practice. The ability to set boundaries matures over time.

Several things tend to happen when you begin to set boundaries by saying no.

First, the more you say no, the less guilt you will feel when you say it. You will feel increasing strength and confidence that you can make good choices for yourself—choices that free you to say yes to those things that truly nurture your inner self, that are productive and beneficial to yourself and to others, and that are in alignment with your life purpose.

Second, when you say no to people who are critical, unloving, or overly demanding, you likely will discover that they stop asking things of you, or stop spending their time and emotional energy on you. Emotional bullies tend to like easy targets. When you put up resistance with a no—and especially a no response that is linked to what you will do if a person fails to heed you—an emotional bully tends to walk away and find a different target.

If you are having difficulty saying no, start by saying it to simple things that don't involve others. Say no to that second helping of food. Say no to the temptation to shop rather than walk at the indoor mall for exercise. Then, begin to say no to the stranger or acquaintance who places unnecessary demands on your time or attention. Say no to the person who calls you at dinnertime and asks, "Is this a good time to talk?" Say no to the salesman who knocks on your door and wants you to buy products that you don't need or want.

You may want to add a phrase to your no so that you don't feel rude. You might say:

- "No, thank you."
- "No, not at this time."
- "No; I don't feel led to undertake that at this time."
- "No; I can't accept your kind invitation right now."
- "No; I have already made another commitment." That commitment may be to yourself. It may include taking a long bubble bath or curling up in front of your fireplace with a good book!

SUBMISSION IS NOT AN AUTOMATIC YES

Some people assume that submission is equal to saying an automatic "yes" when anything is asked of them. Some people who hold positions of authority believe that a person who is truly submissive is at their beck and call, always available, always willing, always capable of providing help, and under their full control and power.

That isn't at all what submission means or involves.

Submission must be understood in context. If practiced according to God's design, submission is for your safety, not your harm. It is not to control you, but rather to protect you. You will see that as you study what the Word of God says about submission.

The Bible tells us that we are to submit ourselves to one another in the fear of God—fear in this case referring to an awe of, a reverence for, or respect for God (see Ephesians 5:21). In other words, we submit to God in worship and service to Him, and as we submit to God, He enables and empowers us to submit to others as a form of ministry to them.

What does it mean to submit, then? It does not mean to cave in or to become a doormat for another person. It means that we are to humble ourselves and get out of the way. In plain language, we bow out. We yield the right-of-way. When we submit to God, we offer God full reign to do what He desires to do in any given situation. We yield our will to His and give Him the total right-of-way to accomplish what He desires to accomplish in us, through us, and around us.

When we submit to another person, we allow that person to make a choice or decision, voice an opinion, undertake a task, do a job, or express an emotion with full freedom of expression, full personal responsibility, and full exercise of God-given talents. We freely let her exercise her free will!

This means, of course, that at times we might be giving another person an opportunity to make what we consider to be a bad choice or a wrong decision. We might find ourselves giving another person an opportunity to take a risk and possibly fail. We might find ourselves giving another person an opportunity to make a mistake and learn from it.

This is hard! No parent wants to see her child try and fail—but every parent knows that unless she allows her child to try and fail, that child will never learn to walk, feed himself, or succeed at anything in life. Making personal choices and reaping the consequences of those choices are vital for maturing.

SAYING NO TO ANOTHER PERSON CAN BE SAYING YES TO YOURSELF

We tend to think that if we say no to someone we will be hurting that person's feelings. There are people who find that saying no brings them personal pain. It feels as if saying no is an admission that they are shirking responsibility, admitting weakness, or limiting their own ability to make a contribution. I know. I have personally experienced this at different points in my life, when I had to pull away and carefully set healthy boundaries.

For most of my life, I considered myself to be the "make-it-happen" girl. If my boyfriend, brother, or one of their friends needed to be cleaned up after a few too many drinks, I did the dirty work. If my mother needed help getting to bed after falling asleep on the couch, I was the helper, even as a child. Most of my friends expected me to take a leadership role in whatever activity we did. Whether this expectation was articulated or not, it always seemed to evolve that way.

Then I encountered a situation where I could not make anything happen. I felt that there wasn't a word I could say that would fix things. There wasn't a sermon I could preach, a letter I could send, a check I could write, or a call I could make. It was a time when many things I considered to be a "sure foundation" were shaken. The "make-it-happen" girl couldn't make *anything* happen! Only God could.

It was during that time that I truly believe my faith graduated to trust. Trust is when you rely upon God completely to make all things happen in your life and in the lives of others. You aren't just believing with your faith for *something*; you are trusting God for *all things*.

There are times when the best thing you can do for others, and for yourself, is to admit that there's nothing you can personally do to change a situation.

> There are times when the best thing you can do for others, and for yourself, is to admit that there's nothing you can personally do to change a situation.

We each need to learn how to live in trust. Ultimately, none of us can make anything happen. All we can do is have an influence, either for good and for God or for evil. And the primary person you can influence is yourself.

I'm not advocating that you sit down and wait for eternity's bus to roll by. What I am saying is that you must do what you can do, and then trust God to do what only He can do. Some situations are totally beyond your ability to make things happen, or even to have much influence. Accept that reality, and trust God to work in His own unique, mysterious, and awesome ways. You may never know what God does, or how. But you can always stand amazed that He promises to work on your behalf, and does so.

NEVER LIMIT GOD

The boundaries you set are for your good and for the good of others. Never set boundaries on God. It's futile to try.

When you establish healthy boundaries, you are free to be yourself and the other person is free to be himself. You release enormous potential for love and harmony into your relationship.

When you set healthy boundaries, you are saying to God, "I can't. You can. I trust You to do what You desire to do." You are giving God full permission to do His work in the lives of every person involved.

Invite God into your relationships. Ask Him to guide you in setting boundaries. He'll do it.

21

IDENTIFY KNAPSACKS
AND BOULDERS

*O*ur children are grown and have started families of their own, giving us the most incredible, beautiful gift of grandchildren. I was amazed not long ago as I waited for my grandchildren at a school crossing and watched a long line of children cross the street and walk into the playground of the school. Needless to say, it had been a while since I had visited an elementary school. Each child was carrying a huge backpack. I've seen check-in luggage that was smaller. I cringed at the thought of how much weight they were carrying. What a load we require our children to bear!

The Bible contains two words that are very important to a person's understanding about where boundaries and responsibilities need to be set. They refer to the emotional weight we carry in our relationships with other people. The words are *load* and *burden*.

WE MUST CARRY OUR OWN KNAPSACKS

God's Word says that each person shall bear his own load (see Galatians 6:5). This word *load* could also be translated "knapsack." This type of load refers to those things that we carry daily in the routine course of living out our human lives. We each carry a set of thoughts, attitudes, beliefs, needs, possessions, and abilities. We each carry responsibility for our own bodies, character traits, and use of time.

Jesus taught His followers that we each have a "yoke" related to the work we do (see Matthew 11:30). No person is immune from doing certain tasks in life, just as no person is totally immune from being under the authority of some sort of taskmaster. We all are in lines of authority that generate certain obligations and work.

Some of the tasks for which we are responsible are spiritual and emotional tasks. Those who are in Christian circles tend to call these tasks "ministry." Some of the tasks for which we are responsible are personal tasks, such as eating, sleeping, taking care of our bodies, learning the things we need to learn, and doing the work we need to do. Some of the tasks, such as working, abiding by laws, and paying taxes, fall to us because we live in a certain community or nation.

Bob Dylan made a good point when he sang that we each have to serve *somebody*. We each have a yoke. The good news, of course, is that Jesus said His yoke—what He requires of us—is a yoke that truly fits us, doesn't chafe against our God-given identity, and allows us to do what is required of us, efficiently and with tremendous productivity (see Matthew 11:29–30).

The principle is this: you are responsible for carrying your own knapsack or yoke.

You are responsible for what you adopt as opinions and beliefs.

You are responsible for what you take into your mind—what you learn and what you do with that knowledge. You are responsible for what you take into your thought life—what you read, watch, or study. You are responsible for the fantasies that you develop and the dreams that you cultivate.

You are responsible for the talents God has given you, and for the way in which you develop those talents into practical skills.

You are responsible for what you believe. Parents and teachers may have passed on a good set of beliefs to you. (If so, thank God for their influence on you, and take responsibility for living out those beliefs in practical ways and for passing on those beliefs to others.) In other instances, parents and teachers may *not* have passed on accurate truths about the nature of God, your own potential, or the abiding traits of other people. If that's the case, wake up and take responsibility for discovering what you believe and making sure that your beliefs are rooted in truth.

Many people need to unlearn and relearn serious lessons about the nature, or character, of God. Others need to discard and replace serious prejudices against other people. It's *your* responsibility to take charge of what you believe.

You are responsible for how you respond to the needs that you perceive around you—which actually means you are responsible for developing an ability to perceive needs and a capacity to respond to needs. We tend to think of needs as being related to other people, but they are also personal. You are responsible for isolating, identifying, and addressing areas of need—physical, emotional, and spiritual—in your own life.

Face up to your own needs or things you lack. If you need instruction, get it. If you need prayer, request it. If you need wise counsel, seek it out. If you need help, find it. Our world abounds with information and avenues that provide spiritual, psychological, emotional, physical, and financial assistance. Don't live in your need; live in a way that creates a way *out* of your need.

> Don't live in your need; live in a way that creates a way out of your need.

You are responsible for what you put into your body and how you exercise, or care for, your physical being. You are responsible for what you do with the twenty-four hours a day that you are given. You are responsible for the way in which you approach your work, do it, and reflect upon it. You are responsible for setting your own goals and making your own plans for achieving those goals.

Recognizing that you are responsible for those things may bring you to a clearer understanding of what is *not* your responsibility. It most definitely is not your responsibility to carry another person's knapsack.

Let Others Carry Their Own Knapsacks

Allowing another person to carry his own yoke is not selfish on your part; it's helpful!

When we take on the knapsacks of other people, we assume that *we* are responsible for their behavior, their beliefs, the fulfillment of their lives, the development of their talents, and the meeting of all their emotional needs. The person who takes on another's knapsack is choosing to carry what the other person should be carrying for himself.

Not long ago, a friend told me about her travel experience under the security restrictions now in place for air travel. She watched a mother with a baby and three children under the age of ten. The baby was strapped to the mother's body in a knapsack, along with a small satchel in which she had diapers and various other baby-related items. Each of the older children also had a small backpack. As they all emptied their hand luggage to be searched, my friend couldn't help but see the content of the children's backpacks. Each child had a couple of small books to read, a coloring book, a puzzle book, crayons, and pencils. Each child also had a small stuffed animal, a pair of pajamas, a set of underwear, a toothbrush, and a hairbrush.

What a smart mother! Not only was she prepared to take care of her baby, but each of her children was learning how to take care of himself and some of his own possessions. This mother wasn't only traveling efficiently with her children; she was teaching her children how to travel and how to take personal responsibility.

Emotionally and spiritually, we are required by God to do the same. When we attempt to take on the knapsacks of other people, several things are inevitable:

We actually keep another person from maturing or taking personal responsibility (see Ephesians 4:15). In doing for her what she can and should do for herself, we limit her experience, and therefore, her ability to learn from experience. We limit the emotional growth that accompanies taking responsibility for one's own thoughts, words, and deeds.

We become poor stewards of our own energy, strength, time, and talents.
When we take on unnecessary loads, we tax our strength in ways it was
never intended to be taxed (see Matthew 25:14–30).

We are each individually gifted with varying degrees of strength and
energy. This is true physically and emotionally. I personally have a tremendous amount of physical energy. I don't expect others around me to
be able to work as long or as hard in any given day, week, or month as I
do. I've learned through the years that as much as other people may *want*
to increase their strength and energy, there's only so much a person can
do to develop our God-given capacity. We each have a limit to what we
can accomplish, carry, or work at in a given time frame.

We should certainly develop our strength and increase our energy as
much as possible, however. That's what exercise, training, development, and
other growth activities are all about. But we also have a fixed limit. When it
comes to time, we have twenty-four hours in a day. When it comes to physical strength, a small-boned, five-foot-two-inch woman is not going to be able
to develop the same muscle mass as a large-boned, six-foot-two-inch man.

When it comes to emotional strength, we also have a certain individual capacity. The spiritual gifts and ministry roles listed in the New
Testament point toward this truth: we each have unique emotional and
spiritual propensities, and a unique calling to a particular level and type
of leadership (see Romans 12:6–8 and Ephesians 4:11–16).

When we become preoccupied with another person's need to grow
or develop, we inevitably siphon off some of our energy, creativity, and
ability, and in the end, reduce our capacity to become and do what God
has crafted for us. It is entirely possible that we can become so preoccupied with carrying another person's knapsack that we neglect what we are
uniquely gifted and designed to do.

Never lose sight of the truth that your particular knapsack has been
God-designed and God-given. Nobody else has your unique set of talents, gifts, propensities, capabilities, dreams, or desires. Nobody else has
your personality. You are designed to be a one-of-a-kind person, and as a
part of your unique design, you are crafted to carry a one-of-a-kind load.

The more you preoccupy yourself with carrying another person's load, the more you are prone to neglect what *you* are responsible to become and do.

We are in danger of preventing others from fulfilling God's plans for their lives. To carry another person's knapsack can mean that we deprive that person of learning how to pack a knapsack, how to make choices about what to pack, and how to develop the muscle power to carry a knapsack for a long walk. Extend that to the spiritual and emotional realm. In carrying another person's knapsack, you may very well be depriving that person of the opportunity to develop ministry skills or emotional strength, spiritual discernment or earthly wisdom, and spiritual authority or personal growth.

God has given each of us free will with which to make certain choices, including the decision about whether to accept Jesus as our personal Savior. If God—who certainly is capable of governing each person's life in a beneficial way—is willing to grant us the opportunity to make personal choices, who are we to think that we can or should govern another person's life? We must acknowledge the gift of free will in the lives of others and allow other people to make choices for which they are responsible. We might not agree with their choices, but we can respect them, whether good or bad, right or wrong in our eyes.

> We have a responsibility to love others, but not to do for them what they can do for themselves. We are to help others, but never to take on the responsibility of being either their god or their slave.

Yes, we have a responsibility to love others, but not to do for them what they can do for themselves. We are to help others, but never to take on the responsibility of being either their god or their slave.

Every person must be responsible for her own choices, decisions, thoughts, beliefs, words, and deeds.

HELPING WITH BOULDER BURDENS

The second word the Bible uses in describing a weighty load or responsibility is *burden*. God's Word says that we are to bear one another's burdens, and that in doing so, we are doing what Christ commanded (see Galatians 6:2).

Think of a burden as a boulder. A boulder has crushing, oppressive power. If a boulder falls on a person from even a moderate height, it can kill that person. A boulder often is so large it cannot be lifted, carried, or moved by one person. What are the boulders of life? They tend to be crises or emergencies—the flood that washes your home away, the sickness that knocks out the family's chief breadwinner, the automobile crash that puts an entire family in the hospital, and so forth. Life has boulders! And when we see a situation in which someone is struggling under a crushing blow—physically, emotionally, materially, or spiritually—by all means, we are to help that person to the full extent of our ability.

The carrying of boulders, however, is not an ongoing task or responsibility. We are to help move boulders out of people's way, and then let them get on with their lives.

Boulder-moving is short-term work. It is never an ongoing responsibility.

Boulder-moving also nearly always requires teamwork.

Boulder-moving is usually very practical. It may mean arranging a doctor's appointment for someone, or launching an effort to rally financial help to pay a large medical bill. It might mean getting someone a job, or helping a person clean up a damaged home.

Boulders and knapsacks require far different responses.

KNOW THE DIFFERENCE

Become an expert at recognizing the difference between a knapsack "load" and a boulder "burden." Carry what is yours to carry. Help others with their major burdens, and recruit additional boulder-movers to assist you with yours.

Ultimately, of course, we must take all loads and burdens to God. Ask for His help. He can remove, lift, release, and shift loads for your benefit as no human being can!

22

SET HEALTHY BOUNDARIES
IN YOUR FAMILY

*E*very child is concerned with "turf." One of the first concepts every toddler nails down is summarized by the word, "Mine!" There's very little sharing and very little empathy in a toddler. And in some cases, toddlers spend a lot of energy on tears and tantrums in an attempt to get what they think is theirs! If you are a parent, you know exactly what I'm talking about.

The process of learning what is rightfully yours and what rightfully belongs to someone else is just that—a *process* of learning that occurs over time.

Boundary-setting is first learned in families—whether those boundaries are healthy or not.

In a healthy family, each child feels attached to the other members but also becomes increasingly independent as he matures in his thoughts, beliefs, and personal choices. A state of interdependence, but *not* codependency or total dependency, is developed within the family. In interdependence, each person learns how to make healthy, responsible choices. There are at least seven marks of a family with healthy personal boundaries:

1. *Each person's opinion is heard.* Each person feels safe to disagree with other family members without experiencing rejection, isolation, or criticism. Each person is encouraged to think, reason, and learn—and to develop personal opinions without censure.

2. *Each person is encouraged to express her emotions in healthy ways* that do not bring injury to other family members, without ridicule or embarrassment.

3. *Each person is encouraged to discover her unique gifts and talents,* and to develop them to the fullest.

4. *Each person is given age-appropriate freedoms of choice*—such as choices about clothing, food, hobbies and activities, courses in school, and friends.

5. *Each person is respected* as a member of the family and is shown courtesy.

6. *Each person is encouraged to be quick to ask for forgiveness and to freely forgive.* No one in a family is right all the time, and it's never right to withhold forgiveness or to fail to ask for forgiveness when wrongs are committed.

7. *Each person is encouraged to pray at family gatherings—such as meal-times—but no one is forced to pray.* Respect is shown for each person's personal relationship with God.

Giving a child the freedoms above does not in any way diminish a parent's right, privilege, and responsibility to provide guidance, direction, prayer, or influence. Neither does it limit parents in establishing family rules and guidelines. As one mother put it, "I don't cater to the food choices of each of my three children—if I did, I'd be making three menus' worth of food at every meal. But I do give my children the privilege of not eating certain foods that I set before them. I ask only that they try certain recipes or foods so they truly will know whether they like them or not."

A LIMITED NUMBER OF OPTIONS

One of the best ways to train children to make wise choices is to set before them a limited number of options. For example, a parent might say to a child in a restaurant, "You may have this, or this, or this." When shopping for school clothes, the parent might let the child choose one or two outfits from a limited selection of items. The parent is the one who makes decisions related to the flow of money in a household, but a parent may give a child an allowance so he can make purchasing choices and decisions in age-appropriate categories.

Limiting the options is a good guideline for many choices and decisions that a parent might set before a child. One child may want to take music lessons; another may want to take ballet. One son may want to go out for the football team; another may want to be part of the chess club. One daughter may want to wear jeans to school, another a dress. Allow your children to make choices—but again, within limits. Certainly there must be limits to the numbers of extracurricular activities a school-aged child pursues. As one person put it, "There are only so many directions the family car can go in a given day." But do allow your children to have a strong sense of their own individuality and decision-making power.

At the same time, choose to make some decisions as a family whole, such as where the family will vacation next summer, what fun event might be scheduled for Saturday afternoon, which ministry outreach the family might undertake together, or how household chores might be divided and assigned.

The healthiest families are those in which the mother and father are interdependent in their marriage relationship—each giving the other the seven marks of respect and freedom identified above. Children learn good, healthy behavior when good, healthy behavior is modeled for them.

WHAT HAPPENS WHEN HEALTHY BOUNDARIES AREN'T SET IN A FAMILY?

A child who grows up in a family where good boundaries aren't set is vulnerable to both emotional injury and confusion about boundaries. Perhaps most injurious of all is that a child can grow up without understanding who God created the child to become and the good fruit that the child is capable of producing.

That child might also experience:

- Undue pressure and responsibility in caring for other family members, such as misplaced feelings of responsibility for the actions of parents (including alcoholic, emotionally ill parents)
- A damaged sense of ownership—not really knowing what belongs to him and what does not
- A false perception about right and wrong—equating disagreement with sin, and confrontation or debate with guilt
- Pent-up anger
- A fear of showing emotion
- An inability to properly evaluate consequences for specific behaviors

In the end, a child who doesn't understand healthy boundaries can find himself tremendously confused when it comes to who he is and how to relate appropriately to other people. The child says yes to things that are not his responsibility or privilege, and no to things that are rightfully his.

Growing up with boundary confusion nearly always results in at least one of these conditions by adulthood:

1. Extreme dependence. When an adult is extremely dependent upon others, he usually manifests an excessive desire to please them and feels great guilt or fear when he believes he hasn't done so. The overly dependent person gives up personal responsibility as he seeks to please others—often blaming others for personal failures. He cannot set limits and tends to live with great confusion, frustration, and anxiety because he never knows when he has done enough or hasn't tried hard enough. The overly dependent person rarely has personal goals and has very little direction for his own future. This person is likely to say, "Nobody is helping me in the way I need to be helped."

The emotionally healthy person does his best to please others, but if his best efforts don't match the other person's expectations, he does not blame himself for the failure or feel guilty. He simply concludes, "I have done my best to please a person who cannot be pleased by my best effort."

2. Extreme independence. Some adults who have boundary confusion have great fear of abandonment because they aren't sure of the extent to which they are supposed to take care of themselves, and the degree to which others should be involved in an interdependent relationship. To avoid being abandoned, the person with avoidance behaviors will deny certain God-given needs. He may become very independent, refusing to trust others to get close. He may be afraid to ask for help, or he may feel guilty about asking for help. At the same time, he often expects others to read his mind and to offer the help that is needed.

Those who live at the extremes of dependence or independence are prime candidates for codependency. Codependent relationships are those in which at least one person in the relationship puts boundaries where no boundaries should exist, or fails to put boundaries where boundaries should be in place. Codependency often leads to addictions and depression.

The emotionally healthy person does her best to care for another person who is in need—especially focusing on physical needs—but does not feel emotionally responsible for the other person's happiness.

3. Controlling behaviors. The adult with confusion about boundaries often attempts to carry the knapsack of everybody he encounters. He starts out trying to help and ends up controlling. He often projects his own sense of extreme responsibility onto others. He very often has little regard for another person's space or schedule. He intrudes quickly, without even recognizing that he is intruding. He may exploit others in the process of attempting to control or overly "help" them. He has difficulty hearing "no" from others. At the same time, he does not take ownership of his own actions. This person may say with frequency: "I don't have time for myself because I'm so busy taking care of other people and meeting their demands."

The emotionally healthy person allows others to take personal responsibility for how they organize their own space and schedules. In turn, she takes responsibility for her own space and time management.

4. Narcissism. The narcissistic adult grew up not understanding that all relationships involve some forms of negotiation, compromise, and give-and-take. As a result, he becomes all *take* and no *give*. He sees the world as revolving around himself, with no consideration for others. He ignores the needs of others and gives virtually no help to those who are dealing with boulders in their lives. The Bible speaks of those who "withhold good" (see Proverbs 3:27). The narcissist is such a person.

Boundary confusion ultimately is a matter of not knowing what you are responsible for emotionally, and the degree to which other people are responsible for their own lives.

I've identified extremes, but the reality is that all of us have questions about boundaries from time to time. Even the best of parents asks herself, "Did I do everything I should have done for my child?" or "Did I limit my child in some way?" Even the best of spouses asks himself, "Am I doing enough to create growth and nurture a loving, respectful marriage for my spouse?" or "Am I causing my spouse to become lazy, overly dependent, or stuck in a rut?" We ask these same questions about our relationship with elderly parents, friends, and grandchildren. And if we are truly going to confront our boundary issues, we also must ask questions of *ourselves*. Ask yourself:

- Am I taking time for myself? Why or why not?
- Do I nurture, protect, and stay true to my authentic self?
- Am I limiting myself by taking on unnecessary responsibilities for others?
- Do I have interdependent relationships with others? Am I codependent, overly independent, or overly dependent?

When you learn to set healthy boundaries and live in healthy interdependent relationships with other people, you model good boundary-setting to your children and to others who watch your life. You teach by example as much as by direct instruction.

If you are a parent today, you have a tremendous responsibility, but also an awesome opportunity, to impact our future as a nation and the future of the church.

Good boundaries are critically important to emotional and psychological health. They are critical to good marriages and friendships. They are critical to people's working and living in harmony with one another, without regard to racial or socioeconomic prejudices.

Don't neglect or diminish the importance of doing what God calls you to do in your marriage, your relationship with your children, and the other relationships God ordains in your life. Set healthy boundaries. Teach boundary-setting to your children. Prepare them to become emotionally healthy adults!

23

CLEAR UP BOUNDARY CONFUSION

*N*obody grows up in a perfect family. At least not anybody I know. As long as we remain imperfect people, every family will have some degree of dysfunction, and every parent will make mistakes. The challenge each of us faces is to learn how to overcome that dysfunction and reverse the errors in our own adult lives so we can experience the rich, full, satisfying life God has designed for us.

We may not have created boundary confusion for ourselves, but we do have the responsibility for clearing up the confusion for ourselves.

We must confront why we do what we do for others by examining our history, habits, and motives.

We must confront why we put ourselves last (or first) on the pampering list.

We must ask ourselves if the boundaries we learned or didn't learn as children were the healthiest boundaries a person might have.

RELEARN WHERE THE BOUNDARY LINES ARE

What do you do if you are confused about where boundary lines should be drawn? What do you do if other people tell you that you are too dependent, too independent, too controlling, or too self-absorbed? If you did not learn healthy boundary-setting as a child, how can you learn this as an adult?

CONFRONT THE MYTHS

First, recognize that you may have adopted some myths in your life and labeled them as truth. Nearly every person with boundary confusion has acquired myths about God, about self, and about the appropriate way of relating to other people. Here are just a few of those myths:

Myths about God. "God should answer all of my prayers the way I want." "God should always say yes to me and to what I want." "God should keep me from ever experiencing anything bad." The myth is that God is like a genie in a bottle. The truth, of course, is that sometimes God says no—or "wait for something better"—to our requests because He loves us, not because He hates us. The truth is also that God allows us to go through difficult times—many of which are of our own creation—in order to teach us, train us, redirect our lives toward a more positive goal, help us grow up, or bring us to a realization of our need for Him. God never sends us bad things, but He uses opposition and persecution as opportunities to position us for the life He has designed for us.

Myths about others. "My happiness is somebody else's responsibility." "If I say no to others, I'm selfish." "I'm indispensable to others." The myth is that if we withdraw from someone or rely less on someone, we will hurt that person. The truth is that in many cases, we may actually be helping that person!

Another myth is that other people control circumstances and there-fore, they control happiness. The truth is that even in dire or difficult circumstances, you can have inner joy—nothing outside you forces you to respond with misery or despair, just as nothing outside you forces you to respond with exhilaration and ecstasy.

Speak the truth with compassion and love. Express to the person your belief that he can take greater responsibility for himself. Express hope that as he takes on more personal responsibility, he will become emo-tionally stronger and increasingly more capable of making his own good decisions.

Myths about self. "If I'm needy, I'm bad." "If I love, I must be loved in return." "I'm not responsible for my own life." "If I'm good, I deserve to be loved." The person with boundary confusion tends to believe that he must be perfect or good if he is going to be counted as valuable or lov-able. Sometimes abuse is even perceived as warranted, because a person believes she is bad in some way, and therefore unlovable and deserving of hurt or pain.

The truth is that nobody can truly love another person uncondition-ally. As finite human beings, none of us has the capacity to love uncon-ditionally in all situations at all times. At times we struggle to forgive, at times we find it impossible to reconcile, and at times we establish expecta-tions about behavior from ourselves and others that may not be realistic. As much as we struggle to love *others* and strive to be loved by *others,* we often struggle to love *ourselves* and strive to be whole in our *own* eyes too.

The good news is that God does love us unconditionally. God has the unceasing capacity to forgive and the unending ability to restore. He regards us as worthy, apart from our behavior. He loves us simply because we *are.* He created us and He loves us. Period. God commands us to obey Him, and He desires that we love Him, trust Him, and communicate with Him, but His love is established from the moment of our creation.

> He loves us simply because we *are.* He created us and He loves us.

DIAGNOSE YOURSELF

Ask yourself:

- Do I have difficulty saying no to people I love? Do I have difficulty saying no to people I work with? Do I have difficulty saying no to people in charge of projects for which I have volunteered?
- Do I resent other people because I can't say no to the demands they place on my life?
- Do I feel manipulated, mistreated, or emotionally abused by another person or by several other people?
- Do I feel as if I'm sitting on a powder keg of suppressed anger?
- Do I feel bitter about the amount of time and energy I'm giving to another person or project? Do I feel under-rewarded and overworked most of the time?

If you answer yes to more than one of these questions, you need to learn to say no! You may very well have boundary confusion. Seek wise counsel. Make an effort to learn who you are, why you do what you do, and what God requires and does not require of you.

SEEK WISE COUNSEL

If you don't know how to establish healthy boundaries, seek more information. Get wise, godly counsel. Ask those who do seem to have healthy self-esteem and honorable relationships, and who seem very capable of saying no, if something you are doing is emotionally unhealthy. Sheer awareness that such things as emotional boundaries exist is very often an eye-opening step toward establishing healthy boundaries.

If you are confused about boundaries, spend some time defining yourself, stating what you like, want, feel, need, and enjoy. Include in your definition what you *don't* like, want, feel, need, or enjoy. Identify some of the limits in your life. What *won't* you do?

PRACTICE SELF-RESPECT

To grow in respect for yourself, you must know yourself. The only way you can begin to know yourself is to spend quality time with yourself. Take some time to do things that interest you or that you find enjoyable. The more you respect yourself, the more clearly you will see where your own needs and responsibilities end and where another person's needs and responsibilities begin.

As a part of practicing self-respect, speak well of yourself at all times. Treat yourself as the most valuable person you know. In truth, you are important, valuable, worthy, and lovable. You are all that!

Embrace a Lifetime
of Discovery
and Transformation

24

DARE TO DREAM NEW DREAMS

$\mathcal{S}$omeone once said, "Dreams are ideas with frosting and sprinkles on top."

Dreams set the heart soaring, the toes tapping, and the mind spinning in positive directions.

Nobody knows what you are truly capable of doing except God. Many people do not even realize their own capacity for success or achievement. Your dreams about your future—not the ones in your sleep, but the musings and daydreams you consciously think about—are a wonderful predictor of what might be possible for you. Dreams uncover your untested potential. Dreams reveal what your basic, innate, and often undeveloped talents could be if you only developed those talents.

> Dreams reveal what your basic, innate, and often undeveloped talents could be if you only developed those talents.

Don't be afraid to dream.

Don't be afraid to test your dreams by exploring the talents related to those dreams.

Fred Astaire is a well-known movie star of the past, known especially for his dancing and singing and his leading-man roles in a number of very popular romantic comedies and musicals. According to Hollywood folklore, an early RKO Pictures screen test report on Fred Astaire read, "Can't sing. Can't act. Balding. Can dance a little." Astaire himself said in a 1980 interview that the report actually read, "Can't act. Slightly bald. *Also dances.*" Either way, the RKO screen test was not a positive appraisal of Astaire's talent. Fortunately for RKO, even though the test was "wretched" in the opinion of studio mogul David Selznick, RKO signed Astaire and then loaned him out for a few days to MGM in 1933 for his Hollywood debut. He appeared as himself, dancing with Joan Crawford in a very successful musical film, *Dancing Lady.* The rest is history.

What do you dream of being and doing?

Your first attempts may seem pitiful or small, but the Bible tells us not to despise small beginnings (see Zechariah 4:10 and Jeremiah 30:19). Even marathon winners take baby steps first.

Some people who see me on television today think that I've always been a preacher and teacher. That's not at all true.

Shortly after I accepted Jesus as my personal Savior and began reading and studying the Bible with great concentration and focus, I had a vision in which God impressed on me that one day I would preach and participate in the transformation of nations. I knew that the vision wouldn't come to pass in a day, a week, a month, or a year. I knew it was for the future. But it gave me a dream—a focus—for what I would one day partake in.

Shortly after that vision, I went to the pastor of the church I was attending and told him God had revealed to me a call to preach the gospel. The pastor put a broom in my hand, literally. I became the church custodian, sweeping the floors, polishing the pews, and cleaning the windows. I was thrilled to do these chores. I had a strong sense that I was doing those tasks—which some would consider menial—for the Lord, and I gave Him my best efforts.

After a while, the pastor asked me to take care of the babies during the Sunday school hour. Again, I was thrilled. I love babies, and to think that I could love those babies and change their diapers and rock them to sleep as a "love offering" to the Lord was a blessing to me.

A while after that, the pastor asked me to work with the children. I found it a wonderful challenge to tell Bible stories and teach Bible principles in ways that children could fully grasp, remember, and apply. Along the way, I applied myself to higher education and did some teaching in public schools. Making lesson plans and presenting them was great training in how to organize thoughts and deliver a sermon. I worked as a youth pastor and director of evangelism in a church.

When my family moved to Tampa, Florida, at the Lord's leading, I worked in the "projects"—government housing for the poor. I ministered in practical and spiritual ways there, mostly to the women and children. When we and five other people started a church in a small space we rented in a shopping center, I filled almost every position possible.

It wasn't until years later, when we were invited to tell about our work at a large church in central Florida, that I preached my first full sermon. The pastor asked me, "Paula, can you preach?" I said, "Yes." In my heart, I knew I could. I hadn't, but I knew I could. He said, "Fine. I'd like for you to do some preaching tonight." I think he had in mind that my preaching would last for ten minutes or so. I preached for an hour! And a number of people accepted Jesus as their Savior and were changed by the presence of God.

That night was like a rocket being launched. During the next year I circled the globe three times, preaching to crowds that numbered in the hundreds of thousands.

Why tell you this?

Because I don't want you to be discouraged about where you are right now. God is preparing you for what comes next in your life. He is fashioning and refining you to fulfill the call and plan He has for you.

Nothing of great or lasting value happens overnight, except your decision to accept Jesus as Savior. That decision, which is made in a moment, changes your eternity and is a decision that cannot be stripped away from you by any human being or circumstance. Everything else we do, however, is a process that occurs over time. Every process has growth and development stages, often for prolonged periods of time, prior to an ultimate "harvest." The process from seed planting to harvest can take weeks, months, and—with some plants—years. But the harvest itself can happen in a day!

Identify where you are in the "dream-to-reality" process. Don't allow yourself to become discouraged. Take a look at the long trend of your progress. You aren't where you were. You aren't where you are going. But in most cases, you are closer to your goal now than you were a year ago or five years ago.

Dare to dream the biggest and best dreams you can dream.

Then dare to pursue them.

25

TAKE ON THE CHALLENGE OF CONTINUAL GROWTH

*L*ife's challenges and opportunities never end. Until the day you die, there will always be something new to experience, to learn, and to give. There are new people to meet, new places to go, and new insights to gain. God designed you to be a continual learner, a continual doer, a continual explorer of His creation, and a continual giver. God never authorized a "retirement age" from any of those pursuits!

You should be different today from who you were yesterday. You should be different tomorrow from who you were last month. There should be a constant transformation in your life. If you aren't changing and growing and becoming more than you were, ask what is stopping this flow of growth and development in your life.

Not long ago, an exercise trainer who has worked with some of the top athletes in our nation told me about an experience he had working with one particular client. The trainer offered to drive this athlete to the ballpark. The summer day was very hot, but rather than turn on the air conditioning, the trainer turned on the heat! The trainer refused to allow the athlete to roll down the window or change the temperature in the car. The trainer was perspiring, but he acted cool. The athlete complained all the way to park, and when they arrived, he jumped out of the car and yelled at the trainer, "What were you trying to do to me? Kill me?" The trainer calmly replied, "No. I was trying to get you out of your comfort zone."

"What do you mean?"

"You are so used to coming to the park in your luxury car and jamming with your friends and doing what you've always done that you don't improve. You play at the level you've always played. I want you to get out of your comfort zone so you will work to get to a new and higher level of performance. I want you to feel uncomfortable to the point that you'll seek to pursue your maximum ability—which, by the way, you are still quite a ways from reaching."

The athlete got the message. He started pushing himself beyond his comfort zone. Even he was amazed at how much he improved during the rest of that season.

> God often takes us out of our comfort zones to stretch us.

God often takes us out of our comfort zones to stretch us and expand our capacity. He desires for us to grow in our abilities, to improve in our effectiveness, and to develop stronger character traits.

CHOOSE TO LEARN SOMETHING NEW

There are few things in life more exciting than mastering a new skill or learning something new.

About a year ago, I decided the time had come for me to fully enter the twenty-first century and learn to use a computer for myself. Prior to that time, I had a very simple understanding about how a computer works. I knew people used computers to send electronic mail, do research, and prepare various reports. I could type. But I had never actually learned how to use a computer to full advantage—which means, in this case, to my advantage.

I bought a personal computer for use at home. Now, I make no claims that I learned how to use my computer quickly or without error. But I did learn to use it, in less time than I thought it would take me to learn the basics for sending and receiving mail, writing letters, preparing sermon notes, and doing research.

I even learned how to shop online and download music, and one of these days, I just may conquer skills related to photos, videos, and graphic art—all of which interest me.

I also decided that I needed to be part of some type of formal study in which I was the student, not the teacher. I have taught Bible studies for years—to women, to church groups, to children and teenagers, to specific groups on specific subjects. I needed to be a *student*. As I write this, I am nearing completion of a master's degree in Psychology. My formal studies have enhanced, not detracted from, my ministry. My mind has been stimulated and enlarged in ways I hadn't envisioned when I began studying. How grateful I am to professors who have challenged my reasoning and demanded excellence from me.

LEARN DAILY

Decide that you will learn something new every day. Keep your mind alive. Stay creative.

I made a personal decision some time ago to read at least three newspapers a day. I don't read every word, but I do read every headline, most of the subheads, most of the photo captions, and most of the articles' lead paragraphs. It's amazing what thirty minutes of reading can do to help you in every area of your life. I learn something every day about what God is doing in the world, something about human nature, and something about how people relate to and communicate with one another—all of which makes me better at knowing how to apply God's Word to the real needs in people's lives. Nearly always, these newspapers teach me something practical that makes my daily life easier or better, improves my time management, or makes me a better steward of my money and resources.

I also made a personal decision to learn a new word a day. There are a variety of ways a person can do this, including a number of calendars that present a new word every day, and several good online vocabulary builders.

EXERCISE YOUR MIND

I have watched people I love experience and recover from strokes and brain injuries, some of them quite serious. I have seen miraculous recoveries in people whose brains were severely damaged. I certainly trust God to be the healer in all cases of sickness and injury, but I also know that God is pleased when we do our part to develop ourselves physically and mentally, so that we are in the best shape possible for healing to occur. I have no doubt that God is pleased when we seek to develop our minds and strengthen our ability to think, reason, solve problems and make good choices until the day we die.

Some people benefit greatly from doing various types of puzzles every day or regularly playing certain games that require mental analysis. Crossword puzzles, anagrams, and *Sudoku* puzzles all provide mental challenge. So does playing a game of chess. I learned just recently that there is no end to the different sequences of play possible in chess—in other words, no person can ever play all the possible games from opening move to checkmate in a single lifetime.

Brain "exercise" is one of the reasons I choose to learn new vocabulary words. The more words you know, the more concepts you can convey.

Engage in conversations about ideas. Learn to pay greater attention to detail. Ask questions. Probe the depths of what someone may know about a topic that interests you.

Listen to tapes or CDs, or watch videotapes or DVDs, that are instructional or educational.

Work complicated jigsaw puzzles—ones that challenge your ability to perceive small differences in color and shape.

I recently heard about a woman who was well into her nineties. She had lost much of her sight, but her hearing was still very sharp. Every day, she listened to a newscast and to programs that featured biographies and history. Not only did she enjoy learning from those programs, but she told a friend about a wonderful added advantage: "I never run out of things to think about or to talk about with my friends."

There's no end to what a person can learn. And that means that there's no end to what a person can write or say. Write about what you learn. Pass on what you learn to someone who can benefit from your study of life. Talk about what you learn. And as you do, learn what others know about the subject.

SET NEW LEARNING GOALS

What is it you would still like to learn? If you've always wanted to take an etiquette class, find one and enroll. If you've always wanted to learn how to bowl, go to the local bowling alley and get started.

Now, people may not understand why you want to learn how to bowl, and people may laugh at the idea that you might ever use the etiquette training you receive, just as some people have questioned why I would want to know more about psychology—but so be it! If it's something that burns within you, that's your passion and it's worth exploring.

If you've never had Thai food or Indian food and would like to try these cuisines, go to a restaurant that features them and ask the waiter to recommend dishes to you. If you don't know what to do with the little glass of liquid that a waiter brings to you after a meal course, ask! Don't assume, as I once did, that it's a dipping sauce when it's actually a palate cleanser for the next course.

If you need directions to a location, don't be too proud to ask for them.

If you need instructions on how to make something, do something, or fix something, seek instruction.

There's no glory in ignorance. There's much to be gained by asking questions and seeking answers.

STAY TEACHABLE

I recently read an interesting research document. Older people reported that they were much happier when they kept their minds open to new ideas and were willing to develop new and positive habits, even if their finances were dwindling or their health was declining. Their inward thinking and feeling, in other words, caused them to rise above their outward circumstances. They had the power of choice when it came to how happy they would feel.

Most learning can be pursued free of charge. You don't need to enroll in an expensive school or course. Vast information is available to you—in fact, you can never exhaust all that you might learn from materials checked out or tapped into at your local free public library. You simply need to take the time and make the effort to read, hear, and see what is available on virtually any subject matter you choose.

New habits do not cost anything to develop. They require only determination and discipline. New skills can often be acquired at very little expense. Countless practical skills-based programs are available free of charge in your immediate community. Explore the possibilities.

If you need more inspiration, find a church where genuine inspiration is available routinely. Get involved in a Bible study, book study, or friendship-oriented small group. Learn from the lives, experiences, and insights of other people. Learn from biblical teaching and preaching.

SEEK UNDERSTANDING AND WISDOM

The ultimate challenge in all of learning is not to acquire more degrees or to be able to dazzle someone with your mental prowess, but to be able to *use* what you learn. The application of facts and principles to everyday life is what we call *understanding*. Knowing when, why, and how best to apply principles is *wisdom*.

BE WILLING TO MOVE ON AND MOVE UP

At times, God may lead you to leave certain familiar environments. That certainly was His message to Abraham when He told him to "Get out of this country, and from your kindred and from your father's house, unto a land that I will shew thee" (Genesis 12:1).

Abraham's relatives, still steeped to a great extent in the Mesopotamian culture that worshiped many gods, were a hindrance to Abraham's future. Abraham needed to make a clean break from them before he could move into the fullness of the destiny God desired for him.

You may need to move out of your current neighborhood, or away from friends who ridicule your faith, attempt to manipulate or control your commitment to God, or seek to keep you from serving God fully. There was a time when some of my family members thought I was crazy for spending so much time reading and studying the Bible. They don't think so now, but they did back then! I had to separate myself from their influence for a while in order to do what I knew God was calling me to do.

To stay in the same place and do the same things that you've been doing for years, and yet expect a different outcome, is pure fantasy. If you truly want different results in your life, you are going to have to do some things differently, think differently, and perhaps believe differently. You may need to physically move in order to get emotionally unstuck from the environment that is holding you back.

When the time came for God to judge the wickedness of Sodom and Gomorrah, He sent angels to lead a man named Lot out of the area (see Genesis 19:1–16). The angels led Lot and his family out of the city and said, "Escape for your lives. Don't look back, nor stay in the plain where these cities have been built. Escape to the mountain or you will be consumed." Lot asked for the privilege of escaping to a little city nearby, and the angels granted him that privilege . . . temporarily. Lot's wife disobeyed the orders from the angels, however, and looked back, which means she lingered behind. She was caught and encased by the brimstone that fell from the sky that day and literally became a pillar of salt. The cities were destroyed. When Lot saw the extent of the destruction, he very quickly went up into the mountains to dwell (see Genesis 19:17–30).

Are you living in an environment today that is filled with crime and debauchery and all sorts of evil influence? God may be calling you to move out! Don't delay when God says, "Go."

Are you living on a plain—the same ol' plain on which you've been living for years? God may be calling you to move to a higher level!

God's plan is never that we stay in evil. He provides a way to escape evil.

God's plan is never that we stop growing. He will always set before us a new goal, a new standard, a new level of excellence that He desires for us to pursue. He will present to us new things to learn, new skills to develop, new insights on which to build, and new techniques that can help us accomplish our goals faster and better than in the past.

Mountain climbers have a simple rule: don't look down. Mountain climbers always look up. That's the goal. That's where the mountain climber will find the next toehold, the next crevice on which to put a hand, the next sure place in which to attach a piton, carabiner, and rope.

Don't dwell in your past. Aim for your future.

This doesn't apply only to those who have negative experiences in their past, or who dwell in a negative environment. It applies equally to those who are still reliving their glory days, which for some people are days lived twenty, thirty, or even forty years ago. Don't sit on the throne of old accomplishments. That was then; this is now. Set some new goals and get busy pursuing them.

> Don't dwell in your past.
> Aim for your future.

You can't look in the rearview mirror and focus on your future at the same time.

IMPROVE YOUR STRENGTH AND FLEXIBILITY

Mountain climbing is an extremely strenuous activity. It takes tremendous strength and endurance. Any upward move in your life—toward any goal or the establishment of any new and positive habit—takes strength.

A couple of years ago, I began to work with a physical trainer in order to improve my strength. I have been an athlete all of my life. As a teenager I competed in gymnastics, swimming, and many other sports. I love to run for miles. I know what it is to have strong, well-toned muscles. I also knew at this particular time in my life that I wasn't living in the physical body that I could have or desired to have. I needed greater strength and agility in order to fulfill the many responsibilities and obligations on my jam-packed schedule. So I began to train my muscles to gain strength.

All muscle growth is a process of tearing down tissue, resting, and then building stronger muscle tissue. The process is one that includes pain.

You may have heard the phrase, "No pain, no gain." That's not a good principle in some forms of exercise, where pain can be a signal to stop immediately, but it is a general rule when it comes to building muscle.

I had to learn to embrace pain as I developed my muscular strength. I had to accept my trainer's words that the pain was doing the tearing-down work necessary for the rebuilding work. It was a process that at times became discouraging because the results weren't quick, or always obvious. But I knew deep within that pain meant progress.

In working with people who need greater emotional strength, I've discovered that there nearly always is pain involved in the process of replacing old emotional strategies with new ones. There can be pain involved in leaving behind a part of your past, in moving from a neighborhood where everybody knows your name and your game, in enrolling in a new course or attending a new school, and in taking on the challenge of a new job or a new role in an organization. Change nearly always brings some excitement and some apprehension, and in the process of change, there's nearly always some adjusting. Change, by its very nature, involves some giving up and letting go, and some taking on and learning anew. Change can be painful, particularly when it leads us into unfamiliar territory.

> You cannot bypass the prescribed process if you want to see the desired progress.

There's no shortcut for the process, however. If a person wants to develop muscle, she has to go through the process. If a person wants to develop character, make mental-habit adjustments, or develop emotional strength, there's a process. You cannot bypass the prescribed process if you want to see the desired progress.

In the same way that you can nearly always extend your physical capacity and level of fitness, you can increase your emotional and mental strength and flexibility. Seek out those things that expand your capacity to think new thoughts and explore new feelings.

Emotional strength and flexibility mean an ability to move freely and appropriately in groups of people who have great diversity. It means not being rigid, not feeling frantic all the time, and not feeling defensive. It means not being reactive, but rather, being responsive. Emotional strength comes to the person who is able to stand back, check out all options, and then respond in a way that brings maximum personal health and peace to all parties involved. The emotionally strong person is able to bounce back from a negative emotion quickly.

Being mentally flexible means being able to take in new information and integrate it, and being able to engage in both logical thinking and intuitive thinking. Mental flexibility includes the ability to take in many different points of view and sift them through a filter of faith and truth in order to come to an effective and beneficial decision or solution. Mental endurance means being able to stand firm under pressure and stress, and having an ability to concentrate or focus until a task is completed or a good decision is reached.

Desire a full "range of motion" for your mind and heart! Increase the options you see before you. How? Stretch yourself to encounter new people and to engage in conversations about new topics.

Prejudice makes a person very rigid. When you're prejudiced, you prejudge a person or situation, and it reveals the narrowness of your mind. Make a point of meeting some people who aren't of your race, your culture, or your background. Go places where not everybody is just like you! For some people, that can mean going to a church that has people of many different races or nationalities. For some, it might mean traveling. For some people who live in large cities, it might mean going into a neighborhood just a few blocks away to shop in a store or have a meal in a restaurant.

Embrace the pain associated with the new challenges God sets before you. You may think that you can't walk into that new group and "start over," or that you can't go to that meeting and admit your bad habits or addiction, or that you can't go to that place and admit to the people there that you need a spiritual do-over. The very thought may be painful to you. Embrace that pain. Nobody has ever truly died from embarrassment or from the fear of something unfamiliar.

If something stretches you, it will change you so that you grow in confidence, self-respect, and faith. You may think that you can't stand in front of a group and share your story or sing your song, you can't be part of a group going into the inner city to help the women and children there, or you can't walk into that new store and shop with confidence. Embrace the pain. Stretch!

The real question is very often this: "Will you trust God to help you?" You don't do anything totally alone. You may not have another human being to stand by, but you always have God by your side. He has promised never to forsake or reject those who trust in Him (see Deuteronomy 4:30–31 and Hebrews 13:5). If you are willing to trust God, you can go into any situation, any place in the world, and be yourself and give what you have to give.

ACCEPT GOD'S CORRECTIVE MEASURES

From time to time, God will prune you, correct you, or teach you new lessons that may seem harsh to you. Accept His correction as being for your greater productivity and growth. Accept His correction as part of a bigger healing process in your life.

A friend of mine was in an automobile accident and the bone in her lower arm was shattered—not just broken, but shattered. There is no simple setting of a shattered bone. My friend went through several surgeries as the bones in her arm fused and healed. In each surgery, areas of the bone needed to be broken and reset so that they could heal in proper alignment. Some healing had to happen before some breaking could occur, and some breaking needed to happen before ultimate healing could occur. In the end, because of the surgeries and repeated breaking of the bone, she gained full function of her arm. She bears a scar, but she has full mobility and strength to do what her arm was created to do.

There are times when we are shattered as human beings. The abuse or the loss is so great that everything in our lives seems shredded. There is no simple fix for that degree of injury. Some healing needs to occur, and then some breaking, and then some more healing, and then perhaps more breaking, and so on, until God fully restores us and we can function with freedom and strength.

Recognize that this is the process God is using to bring you to a life of complete authenticity.

GIVE YOURSELF THE REST THAT PRODUCES CREATIVITY

Just as rest is important to both the body and to our emotions, rest is critical to good mental function.

Recognize how you think. Once you understand a little more about how you think, you will understand better why you need to develop an ability to rest your mind.

Robert Sperry, a neurosurgeon, won the Nobel Prize in 1981 for identifying the behavioral traits associated with the two hemispheres of the brain. The two halves of the brain operate independently of each other, but integration of the two halves is possible and desirable. His right-brain, left-brain theory is well-known today. The left side of the brain has the centers for language, time consciousness, and logic. Those who are left-brained are linear and sequential in their thinking, and they tend to see all of the discrete parts of a process. Left-brained people have an ability to compartmentalize their lives.

The right side of the brain is the creative side. Those who are right brained tend to be visual and to see things as "wholes." They are less linear or time-focused. They tend to solve problems by intuition rather than logic.

The left side of the brain functions mostly at the level of consciousness. The right side of the brain tends to function at a subconscious level.

The two halves of the brain are linked by special neurological pathways. Interestingly, women have many more of these pathways than men.

In today's terms, women are high-speed Internet and men are dial-up when it comes to multitasking.

The creative process has several steps to it that involve both sides of the brain:

1. Insight (right brain—recognizing intuitively a concern or problem, a moment of "inspiration")
2. Saturation (left brain—gathering information)
3. Incubation (right brain—mulling over)
4. Illumination (right brain—breakthrough thinking)
5. Verification (left brain—analyzing)

The person who is fully functioning mentally is able to engage actively in left-brain thinking, but also give the brain rest so it can process information in peace.

How do we give our brains a rest? No one can totally turn off brain activity. Our brains process information even when we sleep. We can, however, "switch channels." We can engage in right-brain activity, and in so doing, give the tedious data-analyzing sides of our brains a rest.

Some of the best ways are to actively engage in right-brain activity are:

Visualization. Close your eyes and take a mental vacation. See yourself someplace beautiful; hear the sounds and inhale the scents of that place. Take a five- or ten-minute excursion into patterns of color and shapes that are beautiful to you. Many people benefit by creating a special "escape room" in their minds.

One woman who has done this for years described her special room to me:

> I walk up a staircase that has shallow, deeply-carpeted steps, until I reach the top of the staircase and go through a wide-open doorway into a room that has a nearly 360-degree view of majestic

mountains, dotted with small pastures, and a river that flows into a lake. The room has a rich hardwood floor and a thick carpet next to the only seat in the room, a very comfortable loveseat and ottoman. A small flowing plant and a table with a stack of beautifully bound books are next to the loveseat. Those are the only items in the spacious room. This is *my* room, and I have total control of all that goes on it. I can turn on lovely classical music to fill the space, or have silence. I can stare at the beauty outside the clear, nearly invisible windows, or read one of the books. The choice is mine. Sun fills the room and at times, giant puffy white clouds sweep overhead, clearly visible through the crystal ceiling. At other times, I imagine a rainy day that turns the entire room into something of a cocoon. At still other times, I imagine the room at night, with stars brilliant above my head and the moon rising from behind a mountain peak. My room is safe and altogether pleasant. If I call for room service, it is immediate, and whatever I order is delicious and satisfying.

What does your "escape room" look like?

Meditation and contemplation. Read a passage from the Bible or an inspirational book, and then close your eyes and imagine that scene in your mind. See the characters. Hear their interaction. Think about how those characters and how their words might play out in a scene from your life.

Gardening or flower arranging. Focus your energies on natural beauty—again, concentrate on the visual aspects of your work. Enjoy the feel of the materials in your hand, even the soft petals of the flowers.

A long, leisurely walk. Although I am all in favor of brisk walking and running for exercise, there is also a great deal to be gained by a long, leisurely walk in a beautiful setting. Stop periodically to give your full attention to a scene you find beautiful. Explore every aspect of the landscape or seascape before you.

A relaxed drive in the country. Take a drive into the countryside, choosing to travel a mostly untraveled road, especially one that might be labeled a "scenic route." Take your time and follow your nose. You might take a picnic basket with you. Stop periodically to sit and gaze at what you see before you. You may find yourself encountering new birds or other wildlife you've never really watched before. Enjoy God's handiwork, His landscape artistry, and His creation of birds and animals.

Playing music or working on an art project. Sink your hands into moist clay or finger paints. Practice a musical instrument. Start with an open canvas and paint, or stitch, or whatever you want—you don't have to be skilled or trained. Enjoy the feel and smell of the paint. Enjoy the tactile feel of the yarn or embroidery floss that you may be working with. A number of women in recent months have told me about their experiences in knitting. They claim it is better for relieving stress than anything else they've discovered. In many cases, women I know are meeting together with other women to knit and talk, and take occasional breaks for a cup of tea. What they are doing is both relaxing and productive. In some cases, the women are knitting baby blankets for poor mothers and their children in the United States and in other nations.

What most people find is that if they give their conscious "left brains" a periodic rest, they are much more creative and productive mentally than if they attempt to work nonstop at figuring out a problem or tackling a complicated project. Be consistent in giving yourself mental breaks. Your overall mental energy will be higher.

The more creative you are, the more outlets you will find for expressing your authentic self.

REWARD YOURSELF GENEROUSLY AND OFTEN

This is vitally important as you seek to build new habits into your life. Stop to say, "Way to go!" to yourself. Say the words aloud. Give yourself a verbal pat on the back.

Give yourself a treat when you reach a milestone goal. Just be sure to treat yourself to something that isn't counterproductive to the next stage of that goal. (In other words, don't reward yourself for losing five pounds by ordering an extra-large deluxe pizza.)

Make a list of things to do, then boldly mark them off as you do them. Use a red pen or some other bright color. Draw a smiley face next to what you have accomplished. Find your own methods and rhythm for rewarding yourself and celebrating your accomplishments.

We tend to return to what pleases us. We like compliments, acknowledgment, and praise. Even if you are the only person praising your accomplishment, give voice to that praise. You'll be motivating yourself forward to further accomplishments. Don't wait for another person to give you the recognition you deserve. Recognize your own achievements and reward yourself!

GO BEYOND YOURSELF TO BENEFIT OTHERS

The end goal of the self-discovery process is not to sit alone and stare into the mirror of your soul, day in and day out. On the contrary! The end goal of locating yourself is to give away the authentic *you*—to use your talents and abilities to benefit others and to bless a needy world. Remember, you have been blessed to be a blessing!

Years ago, I was counseling a woman and her husband. I listened for about an hour to their story. They had been hurting each other for years—each in his or her own way—and they were "beat-up" and in pain. They had been to a variety of counselors and still couldn't seem to find a way to live together in peace and mutual love, respect, and support. Finally I said, "Enough. Here's what I want you to do. Pray. Give it over to God. And get busy." Then I added, "Meet me here on Saturday at noon."

> The end goal of locating yourself is to give away the authentic *you*—to use your talents and abilities to benefit others and to bless a needy world.

They were frustrated at what I said and started hemming and hawing at me. I interrupted. "Pray. Pray separately and if you can, pray together. Ask God to help you. Then quit talking about your problems and trust God to give you His answer. God's got work for you to do. I can introduce you to some of it."

They showed up Saturday at noon, and I took them with me into the inner city. I introduced them to a group of very needy but precious boys and girls. I gave them a challenge: "Find a way of working together to help these kids."

I almost dared them to do it.

They took me up on the challenge, and they eventually became the directors of one of our inner-city projects. Did their marriage improve? Dramatically. Once they quit firing at one another and joined their respective talents to work together on solving a need outside themselves, they discovered each other in new ways. They began to appreciate each other more and to enjoy each other's company. They communicated more freely, not about themselves, but about the needs they saw outside themselves.

I still consider the advice I gave them to be some of the best advice I've ever given:

Pray.

Give it to God.

Get busy.

Eventually you have to quit staring inward and look up and out!

SOMEBODY NEEDS WHAT YOU CAN GIVE

Once when I was going through a very painful series of experiences, I made a deliberate and conscious decision: "I'm not going to sit here in my pain."

I went to a nearby nursing home and asked to meet briefly with the director there. I said, "Tell me the names of the five most needy people in your nursing home. I want to know people who don't have anybody coming to visit them." She not only gave me their names, but she took me to their rooms to introduce me to them.

I devoted a portion of every week to these five dear elderly people, all of whom seemed to be rapidly approaching the end of their lives. I took them soft cookies they could "gum" without dentures, and little bouquets of flowers they could smell even if they couldn't see them. I held their hands and told them stories. I joked with them, and if they were able, took them out to the garden. I listened to their stories of childhood adventures.

Another time when I was feeling low emotionally, I purposefully chose to make regular visits to the hospital. I'd sit out in the smoking lounge closest to the intensive care ward. I don't smoke, and frankly I don't like the smell of smoke, but I knew that the smoking lounge closest to intensive care is where I'd find people who were facing very difficult emotional and stressful situations. Often, I encountered people whose loved ones were close to death after prolonged illness or serious accidents. In many cases, those who were hurting were not only willing but eager to talk. None of them ever turned down my offer to pray for them in a quiet corner of the room.

What did these encounters accomplish? I like to think that I helped the people I found in the nursing home and intensive care smoking lounges. What I know with certainty, however, is that something positive and healthy happened in me as a result of my getting outside of my own pain for a while and encouraging someone else.

When I first began working in the inner city, I knew that each time I picked up a shattered, hurting little girl, I was giving love to a child and in so doing, I was helping that little girl in a way that healed part of me. As a little girl, I needed someone who would hold me, love me, encourage me, and tell me I was special, and I didn't have that affirmation. I saw each child I encountered in the inner city as a "little Paula" who needed what I had once needed. In *giving*, I was *healing* part of my own soul.

I've seen literally hundreds of men and women through the years pour themselves into those who need encouragement, comfort, wise counsel, love, and affirmation. In pouring out their love and time, they are actually healing old wounds deep within themselves. They are refurbishing their own self-value, growing in their own self-respect, and repairing their own damaged self-esteem. They are giving their way into personal growth.

CONCLUSION:
ENJOY YOUR JOURNEY;
ENJOY YOURSELF

*D*on't be afraid to get to know the real you. God made you exactly the way you are and has a unique plan and purpose for your life. Strive to understand who you are, why you do the things you do, and why you think the way you think. Understanding the authentic you is a lifelong journey. Along the way, you will find there are challenges, opposition, mundane moments, times of exhilaration, and seasons of great opportunity.

Keep exploring. Keep learning. Keep asking the tough questions and seeking the best answers. Keep believing. Keep giving and loving and reaching to become all God created you to be.

Enjoy the journey and appreciate the beauty in each moment, realizing that your life is a gift given by God with a specific design unique to you.

ABOUT THE AUTHOR

$\mathcal{P}$aula White, senior Pastor of New Destiny Christian Center in Apopka, Florida (near Orlando), is a renowned coach, bestselling author, and highly sought-after motivational speaker who has been called the "spiritual advisor" to President Donald Trump.

Before becoming President, Donald Trump and Paula had been friends for fifteen years. During that time Paula prayed over him just prior to "most major events" in his life: ahead of a season finale of *The Apprentice* and in the minutes before his speech at the Republican National Convention in 2016. Paula became the first woman to pray at a presidential inauguration on January 20, 2017.

Paula launched her first television show, *Paula Today,* in 2001 and immediately captivated the attention of the American audience. Her viewership soon grew to international prominence due to her ability to connect with people from diverse backgrounds. Media tagged her as "Dr. Phil meets Mother Teresa." Paula has an uncanny ability to reach out in a very real and relevant manner with a heart of compassion, teaching others life principles and success strategies, and at the same time to empower individuals to fulfill their destiny.

Although her early childhood was marred by her father's suicide, and her innocence was stolen by intermittent sexual and physical abuse between the ages of six and thirteen, Paula refuses to be labeled a victim. She continues to press toward the mark of her high calling and has dedicated her life to pulling others out of their crippling circumstances. Each year through various outreach events she touches the lives of the less fortunate, offering hope and encouragement along with practical life-application solutions. "To hold on to your dream and fulfill God's plan for your life, you must keep moving forward," says Paula.

Her current television program, *Paula White Today*, continues her media outreach and commitment to humanity as she reaches out through charities and compassion ministries, always staying true to her core goal of transforming lives, healing hearts, and winning souls.